Robert Foster

ASP.NET 3.5 AJAX

AJAX

UNLEASHED

SAMS | 800 East 96th Street, Indianapolis, Indiana 46240 USA

ASP.NET 3.5 AJAX Unleashed

Copyright © 2009 by Pearson Education, Inc.

All rights reserved. No part of this book shall be reproduced, stored in a retrieval system, or transmitted by any means, electronic, mechanical, photocopying, recording, or otherwise, without written permission from the publisher. No patent liability is assumed with respect to the use of the information contained herein. Although every precaution has been taken in the preparation of this book, the publisher and author assume no responsibility for errors or omissions. Nor is any liability assumed for damages resulting from the use of the information contained herein.

ISBN-13: 978-0-672-32973-9
ISBN-10: 0-672-32973-5

Library of Congress Cataloging-in-Publication Data:

Foster, Robert Hill.
    ASP.NET 3.5 Ajax unleashed / Robert Foster.
      p. cm.
    ISBN 0-672-32973-5
    1. Active server pages.   2. Ajax (Web site development technology)   3. Application software–Development.   4. Microsoft .NET.   I. Title.
    TK5105.8885.A52F67 2008
    005.2'76—dc22
                                                                      2008014763

Printed in the United States of America
First Printing December 2008

Trademarks

All terms mentioned in this book that are known to be trademarks or service marks have been appropriately capitalized. Sams Publishing cannot attest to the accuracy of this information. Use of a term in this book should not be regarded as affecting the validity of any trademark or service mark.

Warning and Disclaimer

Every effort has been made to make this book as complete and as accurate as possible, but no warranty or fitness is implied. The information provided is on an "as is" basis. The author and the publisher shall have neither liability nor responsibility to any person or entity with respect to any loss or damages arising from the information contained in this book or programs accompanying it.

Bulk Sales

Sams Publishing offers excellent discounts on this book when ordered in quantity for bulk purchases or special sales. For more information, please contact

> **U.S. Corporate and Government Sales**
> **1-800-382-3419**
> **corpsales@pearsontechgroup.com**

For sales outside of the U.S., please contact

> **International Sales**
> **international@pearson.com**

Editor-in-Chief
Karen Gettman

Executive Editor
Neil Rowe

Development Editor
Mark Renfrow

Managing Editor
Kristy Hart

Project Editor
Meg Shaw

Copy Editors
Lori Lyons
Karen Annett

Indexer
Erika Millen

Proofreader
Anne Goebel

Technical Editor
Todd Meister

Publishing Coordinator
Cindy Teeters

Book Designer
Gary Adair

Composition
Jake McFarland

Manufacturing Buyer
Dan Uhrig

Contents at a Glance

Table of Contents

About the Author

Rob Foster is an enterprise architect and MOSS MVP in Nashville, Tennessee. He began writing code at the age of 10 when he purchased his first computer, a Tandy TRS-80 Color Computer 2, with money he received for his birthday. He graduated from Middle Tennessee State University with a BBA in Computer Information Systems and holds several certifications, including MCSD, MCSE, MCDBA, and MCT. In 2000 with the PDC bits in hand, Rob founded the Nashville .NET Users Group (www.nashdotnet.org), which is a charter member of INETA. He has been writing and designing .NET applications since version 1.0, as well as implementing SharePoint solutions since SharePoint 2001. In his spare time, Rob enjoys writing books and articles related to .NET and SharePoint. His latest book, which he co-authored, is titled *SharePoint 2007 Development Unleashed*. Rob lives in Murfreesboro, Tennessee, with his wife, Leigh, and two sons, Andrew and Will.

Dedication

To Leigh, Andrew, and Will

Acknowledgments

First and foremost, I would like to thank my wife Leigh for her patience with me writing another book. I signed on to write this book right after our second son was born, and having the support as well as the time to write this book was something that took a lot of sacrifice for our family—and for that, I am eternally grateful. You are the best.

I would also like to thank you, the reader, for continuing to hone your skills. Our industry is ever-evolving, and we have to keep on top of the constant changes that seem to impact our day-to-day working lives. I hope you enjoy the journey of learning ASP.NET 3.5 AJAX, and my goal is that this book can get you where you need to be so you can be a better, more effective developer, designer, and architect.

I can't thank the staff at Pearson enough for making this book a reality. There are a lot of people involved in everything from executing the book contract, authoring, editing, reviewing, printing, and getting the book to bookshelves. First, I would like to thank my acquisitions editor, Neil Rowe, for taking a chance on me and continuing to let me write for Pearson. Other people that contributed from Pearson include Mark Renfrow, Meg Shaw, Lori Lyons, Anne Goebel, and Todd Meister.

None of this would have been possible without all the talented people I have the privilege of working with every day. These are some of the most talented people in the world, and I am very lucky to have these people on my team: Alex Batsuk, Leigh Ann Watkins, Gary Kelley, Richard Brown, Todd Wiser, Matt Wilson, Mike Houston, Tobias Gunn, Mike Anderson, Jaron Jackson, Diane Easter, and Allan Cytryn.

Finally, I would like to thank my cohosts of the SharePoint Pod Show (http://www.sharepointpodshow.com), Nick Swan and Brett Lonsdale. We have a lot of fun doing the show, which helps break up the seriousness of our day jobs. These guys continue to inspire and drive me to be at my absolute best, including finishing writing this book!

We Want to Hear from You!

As the reader of this book, *you* are our most important critic and commentator. We value your opinion and want to know what we're doing right, what we could do better, what areas you'd like to see us publish in, and any other words of wisdom you're willing to pass our way.

You can email or write me directly to let me know what you did or didn't like about this book—as well as what we can do to make our books stronger.

Please note that I cannot help you with technical problems related to the topic of this book, and that due to the high volume of mail I receive, I might not be able to reply to every message.

When you write, please be sure to include this book's title and author as well as your name and phone or email address. I will carefully review your comments and share them with the author and editors who worked on the book.

Email: feedback@samspublishing.com

Mail: Neil Rowe
Executive Editor
Sams Publishing
800 East 96th Street
Indianapolis, IN 46240 USA

Reader Services

Visit our website and register this book at informit.com/register for convenient access to any updates, downloads, or errata that might be available for this book.

Introduction

As an ASP.NET web developer in today's market, you need countless skills to distinguish yourself from the next person. One of those skills that you can quickly acquire is developing AJAX-enabled applications. As your users begin to utilize AJAX-enabled sites on the web, such as Live.com and Google Maps, they are beginning to expect the same rich functionality in the applications that you deliver.

Although these applications took many man hours to create, the process is made easier for you as a developer with the AJAX library that's packaged with ASP.NET 3.5. You can save many hours and lines of code by learning and leveraging ASP.NET AJAX to create and deliver a very rich user experience in your applications.

In this book, you learn how to make the most of ASP.NET AJAX by building on the knowledge that you already have as an ASP.NET developer and extend that knowledge so that you can easily create AJAX-enabled applications. The book has been divided into the following chapters:

Chapter 1—Introduction to AJAX Technologies

In this chapter, you learn the fundamentals of AJAX by first understanding the XmlHttpRequest JavaScript object, and then building a simple AJAX library for use in your applications.

Chapter 2—Introduction to ASP.NET AJAX

Chapter 2 introduces you to the controls and capabilities that are available in ASP.NET AJAX and serves as a springboard for technologies that are discussed in future chapters.

Chapter 3—The ScriptManager and ScriptManagerProxy Controls

Chapter 3 discusses the core object of the ASP.NET AJAX library: the ScriptManager control. In this chapter, you learn the capabilities of the ScriptManager control and how you can best utilize it in your AJAX-enabled pages.

Chapter 4—The ASP.NET AJAX Client API

In Chapter 4, you learn how to make the most of the ASP.NET AJAX client-side objects that are made available via the ScriptManager control.

Chapter 5—The UpdatePanel and Timer Controls

In Chapter 5, you learn how to use the UpdatePanel control to quickly and easily add AJAX functionality to your ASP.NET web pages. You also learn how to use the Timer control to make asynchronous callbacks from your pages at a specified time interval.

Chapter 6—Advanced Techniques with the ASP.NET AJAX `PageRequestManager` Object

In Chapter 6, you learn some essential techniques that can be used with the ASP.NET AJAX `PageRequestManager` object to save you many lines of code as well as help you create richer user experiences for your AJAX-enabled applications.

Chapter 7—Using the ASP.NET AJAX Control Toolkit

In Chapter 7, you learn about the controls that are available in the ASP.NET AJAX Control Toolkit, which is an open-source, community-based suite of controls for ASP.NET AJAX.

Chapter 8—Building an ASP.NET AJAX Extender Control

Chapter 8 first introduces the concept of creating AJAX-enabled extender controls, and then shows you how to build an extender control that can be used in your applications.

Chapter 9—ASP.NET AJAX and SharePoint 2007

In Chapter 9, you learn how to enable ASP.NET AJAX in SharePoint 2007 and Windows SharePoint Services (WSS) 3.0, and then you learn how to build an AJAX-enabled WSS web part.

Chapter 10—Creating ASP.NET AJAX-Enabled Vista Sidebar Gadgets

In Chapter 10, you learn how to build ASP.NET AJAX-Enabled Gadgets for the Windows Vista Sidebar.

PART I

Introduction

IN THIS PART

CHAPTER 1

Introduction to AJAX Technologies

If you've purchased this book, you probably are interested in AJAX technologies. If you are not familiar with the technology or are new to AJAX, it is important that you take some time and understand where AJAX fits into the big picture of web development. This section helps bring you up to speed with AJAX's place in your web development toolbox.

One problem with the design of web pages (especially ASP.NET web pages) is that to refresh the data on the page, it must postback to the server. This causes the page to flicker while the page is posting, and then the page is reloaded in the browser with the results of the post. You can view the amount of data with tools such as IEHTTPHeaders and HTTPWatch. You will quickly notice that the amount of information getting posted is quite sizeable because ASP.NET applications not only postback the controls, but also post the page's ViewState. Although the technique of a postback works, it creates a lot of traffic over the wire and inherently reduces the overall scalability of your application.

Asynchronous JavaScript and XML (AJAX) is a development pattern that you can use to provide your users with a much richer user experience in your web applications. Simply stated, AJAX allows you to asynchronously load data into pieces of a page on demand instead of loading the whole page each time data is requested.

An example of where a user experience can be enhanced by AJAX is a web page that contains related dropdown boxes. For example, say that you have a web page that supplies information on cars in which a user must select the year, make, and model of his car from dropdown boxes on the page. When a user selects a year, she populates all makes for a selected year in the make dropdown box. Additionally, when a user selects a make of car, the models dropdown is populated with models for a given year and make.

If you use traditional ASP.NET without AJAX, you will probably set the `AutoPostBack` property of your dropdowns to true and the page will postback (and flicker) when your user makes selections on the page.

Conversely, if you use AJAX, data can be loaded asynchronously into the list boxes as the user makes selections on the page. This is much more efficient because only the data being requested will travel in the request to the server, which could be as simple as a query string appended to the end of a page request. Also, the page will not flicker as the user makes selections in the dropdowns because the post actually is happening in the background.

> **NOTE**
>
> An example of AJAX is described later in the chapter.

AJAX and Web 2.0

Web 2.0 is a term (or rather buzzword) that you often hear when describing most "modern" web sites; however, it shouldn't be a new concept to web developers. Web 2.0 is actually a consolidation of many existing technologies that allows you to provide a rich interactive user experience over the web. Examples of Web 2.0 technologies include, but aren't limited to, the following areas:

- ► Rich Internet Applications (RIAs), which include AJAX, Adobe Flash, Silverlight, and Moonlight
- ► Web services
- ► Blogs
- ► Wikis
- ► Social networking
- ► Social bookmarking
- ► RSS/Atom

Before the Web 2.0 movement began on the Internet, web pages often focused solely on providing the user with data. The user would simply request a page, view the page, request another page, view that page, and so on.

In contrast, the patterns and techniques behind Web 2.0 are all about the user experience with the web: AJAX and web services for rich, efficient user experiences, blogs, wikis, social networking, and social bookmarking for collaboration, and RSS/Atom so that users can "subscribe" to data.

As technologies such as AJAX evolve and are adopted in large scale on the web, Web 2.0 techniques are quickly becoming the expected user experience for the web. Mainstream examples of AJAX include the Google-based applications, such as Google's Maps, Docs, and Calendar, as well as Microsoft-based applications, such as Hotmail, and Windows Live-based applications. As users start utilizing these types of applications in their every-day lives, they will come to expect the same type of functionality in the applications you develop.

Why Use AJAX?

As stated previously in this chapter, you can use AJAX to help provide a rich user experience. Of all the new, cool techniques and technologies that are available in Web 2.0 and rich Internet applications, AJAX is clearly the most widely used today. Should you use AJAX simply because it's cool? The short answer is "No," which is explained in the next section.

AJAX Rationale

Although the user experience that results from AJAX development patterns is a much richer experience, the rationale for utilizing AJAX is the total amount of traffic that is reduced from users accessing your web pages. When you have a web application with a large user base, using AJAX significantly increases the scalability of the application due to the amount of web traffic that is reduced every time a page is loaded.

The following list gives advantages and disadvantages of AJAX:

Advantages

- ▶ Reduced page bandwidth

- ▶ Load page data on demand

- ▶ Service-based approach to web development

- ▶ Rich user experience

Disadvantages

- ▶ Unexpected browser functionality (when the user clicks the back or refresh button)

- ▶ Business logic can exist in the JavaScript

- ▶ Difficult to test with automated tools

Although this book highlights and focuses on the advantages of AJAX, several disadvantages should be noted. The first thing your users will notice is that when they click the refresh or back button in the browser, the page has a possibility of losing its state when the page reloads. This is a result of dynamically loading data on demand (which was one of the advantages of AJAX).

The second disadvantage of AJAX that you will see in the development world is actually JavaScript. You might wonder that if AJAX is initiated from client-side JavaScript, how can JavaScript be a disadvantage? The answer is that JavaScript eventually will be considered a disadvantage for AJAX in your web applications. Over time, you will be quite shocked at the amount of JavaScript that is required (which is an evolution throughout the lifecycle of your application) for AJAX functionality in your application. It will start out very small and clean, but can quickly spiral out of control.

From the architecture perspective, there is not a clean way to reverse-engineer JavaScript into an architecture model. An architecture document will probably define how a page should function, and there could be thousands of lines of JavaScript behind the scenes to enable this functionality. Depending on your environment and Software Development Lifecycle (SDLC), this could become a problem because it is very difficult to validate the JavaScript against the architecture models.

The third (and certainly not the last) disadvantage is the potential difficulty of testing AJAX functionality with automated tools. For example, Visual Studio Team Suite (VSTS) 2005 had limited support for AJAX when creating web tests. This problem was easily circumvented with tools such as Fiddler (http://www.fiddlertool.com/fiddler/), which helps you capture AJAX requests, which then can be loaded into the VSTS Web Test. It is important to note that these issues have been resolved in VSTS 2008.

This section is designed not to scare you away from AJAX, but to create an awareness of things that can affect you and your AJAX development experience. Best practices and warnings are highlighted in upcoming chapters so that you can be aware of the pitfalls that can show up in your applications.

In the next section, you learn the basics of implementing AJAX in your applications.

AJAX: An Example

Now that you understand the advantages and disadvantages of AJAX, it is helpful to learn about the code behind AJAX requests. This section introduces an example of using AJAX and JavaScript Object Notation (JSON).

The XMLHttpRequest Object

The main object behind AJAX is the XMLHttpRequest object. This object exposes functionality that allows you to send and receive data (usually XML-based, but not required) from client-side JavaScript code to a server page.

XMLHttpRequest has six methods, listed in Table 1.1, and seven properties, listed in Table 1.2.

Deep knowledge of the capabilities of the XMLHttpRequest object's properties and methods is required learning for any AJAX developer. At its core, every library that encapsulates AJAX functionality (ASP.NET AJAX, AJAX.NET, Yahoo YUI, and so on) uses the XMLHttpRequest object.

The next section defines a simple AJAX JavaScript library that can be used to make AJAX calls in your web applications.

TABLE 1.1   XMLHttpRequest Methods

Method	Parameters	Description
Abort		Aborts the request that has been made.
getAllResponseHeaders		Returns a string of all response headers.
getResponseHeader	headerName	Returns the value of a given response header.
Open	method, url method, url, async method, url, async, username method, url, async, username, password	Opens the request to a specified URL. method defines the HTTP method that will be used (typically GET or POST). url defines the location of the page that is being requested. async is a Boolean that defines whether the request will be made asynchronously or not.
Send	content DOMString Document	Sends the request to the server. DOMString is the XML that is to be sent as a string. Document is an XML DOM document
setRequestHeader	label, value	Allows you to add a label and value to the HTTP header that is being sent to the server.

TABLE 1.2   XMLHttpRequest Properties

Property	Description
onreadyStatechange	Event handler that is fired when the readyState property changes. This will be a JavaScript function that handles the data that is returned to the client.
readyState	Returns the state of the XMLHttpRequest object. Possible values are 0 = not initialized 1 = open 2 = HTTP Headers received 3 = receiving 4 = loaded
responseText	Returns the complete response as a string.
responseXML	Returns the complete response (if it is XML) as an XML document object.
responseBody	Returns a binary encoded string of the response.
Status	Returns the HTTP status code of the request. HTTP status codes are defined at http://www.w3.org/Protocols/rfc2616/rfc2616-sec10.html.
statusText	Returns the HTTP status description of the request.

A Simple AJAX Library

As a developer, you probably have several (possibly hundreds of) scripts stuffed away somewhere that you reuse to accomplish specific tasks. One such script you can use for making AJAX calls is provided in Listings 1.1 through 1.3.

> **NOTE**
>
> Although this library can be written many different ways, this example contains three JavaScript functions: createAjaxRequest, createHttpRequestObject, and getResponse. Each function is separated into its own listing and described in the next three sections.

LISTING 1.1   createAjaxRequest Function

```
//Section 1
var http_request = false;

function createAjaxRequest(url, parameters) {
```

```
    http_request = createHttpRequestObject();

    if (!http_request) {
        alert('Error creating XMLHTTP object');
        return false;
    }
    http_request.onreadystatechange = getResponse;
    http_request.open('GET', url + parameters, true);
    http_request.send(null);
}
```

This section contains the `createAjaxRequest` function. This method is called when you want to invoke an AJAX request. When this method is invoked, it first makes a call to `createHttpRequestObject` (described in Listing 1.2) to create an instance of the `XMLHttpRequest` object. After the object is returned, you need to do some error checking around this object to ensure that it was created correctly. Next (and most importantly), the object is configured by setting the `onreadystatechange` property to the `getResponse` function handler (described in Listing 1.3), and the request is opened (as asynchronous) and finally sent to the server.

LISTING 1.2   createHttpRequestObject Function

```
//Section 2
function createHttpRequestObject(){
    var request;
    if (window.XMLHttpRequest) { // IE7, Mozilla, Safari, etc.
        request = new XMLHttpRequest();
        if (request.overrideMimeType) {
            request.overrideMimeType('text/xml');
        }
    } else if (window.ActiveXObject) { // IE 6 and previous
        try {
            request = new ActiveXObject("Msxml2.XMLHTTP");
        } catch (e) {
            try {
                request = new ActiveXObject("Microsoft.XMLHTTP");
            } catch (e) {}
        }
    }
    return request;
}
```

This section contains a helper function called `createHttpRequestObject`. Unfortunately, depending on the type of browser that you are using, there are many ways that you can (or should) create an instance of XMLHttpRequest. This method creates and returns the object instance of XMLHttpRequest that your browser supports.

LISTING 1.3   getResponse Function

```
//Section 3
function getResponse() {
  if (http_request.readyState == 4) {
    if (http_request.status == 200) {
      var xmldoc = http_request.responseXML;
      alert(xmldoc.xml);
    } else {
      alert('There was a problem with the request.');
    }
  }
}
```

Although createAjaxRequest and createHttpRequestObject are somewhat boilerplate functions, the processing of the response occurs in the getResponse function, defined in Listing 1.3, getResponse.

The handler to execute this function was set up in the Section 1 createAjaxRequest method by setting the onreadystatechange property of the XMLHttpRequest object. This function gets fired *every time* the readyState property changes. It important to note that you will not be able to access the response until the readyState property is equal to 4, or loaded, so you first must check the status of the readyState before processing the response.

After your response has been loaded, you must perform another check on the HTTP status. If anything is wrong with your request (for example, 401-unauthorized, 404-page not found, and so on), then you can respond to that error here. In the example in Listing 1.3, the status is checked for a value of 200 (or OK), and then the function will process the request.

As soon as you make these two checks on the readyState and status properties of the XMLHttpRequest object, you can then process the response. In this example, the response is loaded into an XML Document object, and then the XML is displayed in a message box to help confirm the results.

Listing 1.4 is a complete code listing for all of the code described in this section.

LISTING 1.4 Simple AJAX Library–Complete Listing

```
var http_request = false;


function createAjaxRequest(url, parameters, callbackFunction) {
  http_request = createHttpRequestObject();
```

```
  if (!http_request) {
     alert('Error creating XMLHTTP object');
     return false;
  }
  http_request.onreadystatechange = getResponse;
  http_request.open('GET', url + parameters, true);
  http_request.send(null);
}

function createHttpRequestObject(){
    var request;
    if (window.XMLHttpRequest) { // IE7, Mozilla, Safari, etc.
        request = new XMLHttpRequest();
        if (request.overrideMimeType) {
            request.overrideMimeType('text/xml');
        }
     } else if (window.ActiveXObject) { // IE 6 and previous
        try {
            request = new ActiveXObject("Msxml2.XMLHTTP");
        } catch (e) {
           try {
               request = new ActiveXObject("Microsoft.XMLHTTP");
           } catch (e) {}
        }
     }
     return request;
}

function getResponse() {
  if (http_request.readyState == 4) {
     if (http_request.status == 200) {

        var xmldoc = http_request.responseXML;
        alert(xmldoc.xml);
     } else {
        alert('There was a problem with the request.');
     }
  }
}
```

NOTE

You will most likely process the XML document and not display it in an alert. An example of processing the returned XML is explained in the next section.

Using the AJAX Library

After you understand the basics of AJAX, you can start applying this knowledge to your projects. In this section, you learn how to use AJAX to connect two dropdown list boxes in ASP.NET.

This example allows you to select a make of car (BMW, Mercedes, or Porsche) and use AJAX to request the models for the selected car make. The very simple page is illustrated in Figure 1.1.

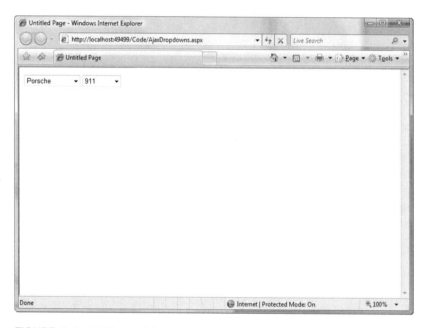

FIGURE 1.1   AJAX dropdowns

When you select a car from the first dropdown, an AJAX request is made to the server to get different car models. For this example, a call is be made to a page called getModels.aspx, which is defined in Listing 1.4.

LISTING 1.4   getModels.aspx

```
<%@ Page Language="C#"%>


<script runat="server">

    protected void Page_Load(object sender, EventArgs e)
    {
        Response.ContentType = "text/xml";
```

```
        string Make = Request.QueryString["make"];
        switch (Make.ToUpper())
        {
            case "BMW":
                Response.Write("<models><car>3-Series</car>
<car>5-Series</car><car>7-Series</car><car>M</car><car>X3</car>
<car>X5</car><car>Z-Series</car></models>");

                break;

            case "MERCEDES":
                Response.Write("<models><car>C-Class</car>
<car>E-Class</car><car>S-Class</car><car>AMG</car></models>");

                break;

            case "PORSCHE":
                Response.Write("<models><car>911</car><car>Cayman</car>
<car>Cayanne</car><car>Boxster</car></models>");

                break;

            case "BLANK":
                Response.Write("<models><car></car></models>");
                break;

            default:
                Response.Write("<models><car>Invalid selection</car></models>");

                break;

        }

    }
</script>
```

This page simply accepts a query string argument called make and will return an XML string of car models, depending on the make argument. A sample of the returned XML where the value PORSCHE is passed into the make query string argument is described in Listing 1.5.

LISTING 1.5   Models XML Records

```
<models>
    <car>911</car>
    <car>Cayman</car>
    <car>Cayanne</car>
    <car>Boxter</car>
</models>
```

NOTE

Note that this syntax is important, because you will learn how to parse the XML document and populate the second dropdown with the values that are returned from this page.

Now that you have learned where the data is coming from, it is time to learn how to request and manipulate the data using AJAX. Listing 1.6 describes a page named AjaxDropdowns.aspx.

LISTING 1.6   AjaxDropdowns.aspx

```
<%@ Page Language="C#"%>
<!DOCTYPE html PUBLIC "-//W3C//DTD XHTML 1.0 Transitional//EN"
"http://www.w3.org/TR/xhtml1/DTD/xhtml1-transitional.dtd">

<script runat="server">

    protected void Page_Load(object sender, EventArgs e)
    {
        //setup the AJAX call on the dropdown
        ddlMakes.Attributes.Add("onchange",
"javascript:createAjaxRequest('getModels.aspx', '?make=' + " + ddlMakes.ClientID +
".value);");

    }
</script>

<html xmlns="http://www.w3.org/1999/xhtml">
<head id="Head1" runat="server">
    <title>Untitled Page</title>

</head>
<body>
    <form id="form1" runat="server">
```

```
<div>

    <asp:DropDownList ID="ddlMakes" runat="server">
        <asp:ListItem Value="blank">Select a Make</asp:ListItem>
        <asp:ListItem>BMW</asp:ListItem>
        <asp:ListItem>Mercedes</asp:ListItem>
        <asp:ListItem>Porsche</asp:ListItem>
    </asp:DropDownList>
    <asp:DropDownList ID="ddlModels" runat="server">
    </asp:DropDownList>
</div>
</form>
<script type="text/javascript">
//Section 1
var http_request = false;

function createAjaxRequest(url, parameters) {
  http_request = createHttpRequestObject();

  if (!http_request) {
    alert('Error creating XMLHTTP object');
    return false;
  }
  http_request.onreadystatechange = getResponse;
  http_request.open('GET', url + parameters, true);
  http_request.send(null);
}


//Section 2
function createHttpRequestObject(){
    var request;
    if (window.XMLHttpRequest) { // IE7, Mozilla, Safari, etc.
        request = new XMLHttpRequest();
        if (request.overrideMimeType) {
            request.overrideMimeType('text/xml');
        }
    } else if (window.ActiveXObject) { // IE 6 and previous
        try {
            request = new ActiveXObject("Msxml2.XMLHTTP");
        } catch (e) {
            try {
                request = new ActiveXObject("Microsoft.XMLHTTP");
            } catch (e) {}
        }
    }
```

LISTING 1.6   Continued

```
            return request;
    }

    //Section 3
    function getResponse() {
      if (http_request.readyState == 4) {
          if (http_request.status == 200) {
              //get dropdown
              var ddl = document.forms[0].<%=this.ddlModels.ClientID %>;

              //clear items in dropdown
              ddl.options.length = 0;

              //get the XML response and loop elements
              var xmldoc = http_request.responseXML;
              var cars = xmldoc.getElementsByTagName('car');
              for(i=0; i<cars.length; i++){
                  //add items to the dropdown
                  try{
                      var opt = new
Option(cars[i].firstChild.nodeValue, cars[i].firstChild.nodeValue);
                      ddl.add(opt, i);
                  }
                  catch (e){
                      ddl.length=0;
                  }
              }
              http_request = null;
          }
          else {
              alert('There was a problem with the request.');
          }
      }
    }

</script>
</body>
</html>
```

As you browse through the code in Listing 1.6, first notice that it is using the simple AJAX library that you learned about earlier in this chapter. You learn about the changes that were made to the getResponse function later in this chapter, but it is important to note because you will also see calls made to the createAjaxRequest function, which is discussed next.

This page contains two dropdowns, ddlMakes and ddlModels, and one server side event handler, Page_Load. When the user selects a car make from the ddlMakes dropdown, an AJAX call needs to be made to populate the ddlModels dropdown with car models. In this example, the AJAX call is set up on the ddlMakes dropdown in the Page_Load event by adding an onchange attribute to the server side dropdown list control and setting its value to call the createAjaxRequest JavaScript method defined in the simple AJAX library.

The big change to the AJAX library is in the getResponse method, which is highlighted in Listing 1.7.

LISTING 1.7   getResponse Method

```
function getResponse() {
    if (http_request.readyState == 4) {
        if (http_request.status == 200) {
            //get dropdown
            var ddl = document.forms[0].<%=this.ddlModels.ClientID %>;

            //clear items in dropdown
            ddl.options.length = 0;

            //get the XML response and loop elements
            var xmldoc = http_request.responseXML;
            var cars = xmldoc.getElementsByTagName('car');
            for(i=0; i<cars.length; i++){
                //add items to the dropdown
                try{
                    var opt = new
Option(cars[i].firstChild.nodeValue, cars[i].firstChild.nodeValue);
                    ddl.add(opt, i);
                }
                catch (e){
                    ddl.length=0;
                }
            }
            http_request = null;
        }
        else {
            alert('There was a problem with the request.');
        }
    }
}
```

As you walk through the method, first, a reference is made to the ddlModels dropdown on the page, and all items are cleared by setting the options.length property to zero. If you don't do this, items will simply get added to the dropdown list every time the user selects a new car make. Next, the XML response is returned from the `http_request` object. Finally, the code loops through the values of all the returned <car> elements and populates the `ddlModels` dropdown list.

When you execute the page, you will notice that the dropdown is populated with data very quickly with no page flicker. This is a great first example of using AJAX because linked (or related) dropdowns are a common scenario that you see in applications. Additionally, functionality such as this is often a developer's first experience with AJAX functionality in their applications.

Before ASP.NET AJAX (and other libraries), this was how we, as a development community, had to write AJAX functionality. One of the first things you will notice about this approach is the amount of JavaScript that you have to write and maintain. It quickly becomes very difficult to maintain and add or change the functionality of your pages without starting from scratch. There is nothing wrong with this approach, and libraries such as ASP.NET AJAX shield you from a lot of the coding and JavaScript maintenance (and the libraries *are* generating this code for you). However, it is important to note the maintenance cost associated with manually writing AJAX code.

Summary

In this chapter, you learned about AJAX and its place in the Web 2.0 world. AJAX has a place in your web applications, and the rationale of utilizing AJAX was discussed in detail as well as the advantages and disadvantages that you will encounter by applying this type of functionality in your applications. Finally, you learned how to build AJAX from scratch using ASP.NET and JavaScript.

CHAPTER 2

Introduction to ASP.NET AJAX

As you learned in Chapter 1, "Introduction to AJAX Technologies," creating AJAX JavaScript is very easy but over time will become difficult to maintain. The ASP.NET AJAX controls and projects make it much easier for you to create and (most importantly) maintain AJAX-based applications. This enables you to provide your users with a very rich user experience (UX) with minimal development effort.

ASP.NET AJAX was offered initially as a separate download that extended the functionality of Visual Studio 2005, but it is now native to Visual Studio 2008 and the .NET Framework 3.5. This inclusion takes the burden off you as a developer to install and maintain a separate component for ASP.NET AJAX.

One of the coolest things about ASP.NET AJAX is that if you currently are an ASP.NET developer, you have most of the skills needed to create AJAX-based applications. Because ASP.NET AJAX is built on top of ASP.NET, you can quickly learn the ropes of ASP.NET AJAX and start using the new AJAX-style functionality immediately in your web applications and pages.

In this chapter, you learn what tools are available to you in Visual Studio; each tool will be explained in greater detail in the chapters that follow. It is important that you understand what is available before you learn how to apply it so that you aren't trying to re-create the wheel when trying to achieve a specific UX in your applications.

Introducing the Visual Studio Controls

Visual Studio 2008 includes a number of new AJAX-based controls that you can use in your web applications. These controls are available for you (as part of the .NET Framework) to either create new AJAX-based web applications or slowly extend the functionality of an existing web application. This section describes each control that is available in the toolbox, as shown in Figure 2.1.

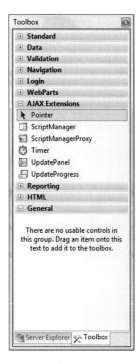

FIGURE 2.1   AJAX-based controls.

ScriptManager

The ScriptManager control is used to manage the generated client-side JavaScript AJAX code on your ASP.NET web pages. It is required for any page that uses ASP.NET AJAX, and only one can exist per page. Additionally, it enables you to quickly implement the following ASP.NET AJAX features on your pages:

▶ Generation of client-side script for ASP.NET AJAX

▶ JavaScript proxy classes for calling web services

▶ JavaScript classes for utilizing ASP.NET AJAX authentication and profile services

▶ Partial-page rendering

The first three items listed are essentially JavaScript helpers that reduce the amount of JavaScript you must write and maintain. This is a major advantage provided to you with

ASP.NET AJAX, as the runtime will help limit the amount of JavaScript that must be maintained in your AJAX-based applications.

Partial-page rendering refers to allowing different "regions" of your page to postback to the server, instead of posting the whole page and its data. The ScriptManager acts as a broker between your page, its regions (usually divided with UpdatePanel controls), and the server-side code that gets called.

ScriptManagerProxy

Because only one ScriptManager control can exist in your page hierarchy (master page, inherited page, and so forth), you might want to define it in an ASP.NET master page to ensure that every page gets this functionality. If you do this, you must use the ScriptManagerProxy class in any page that inherits from the master page so that you can refer back to the original ScriptManager control. ScriptManagerProxy will give you a locally defined object in your page but will get all of its functionality from the referenced ScriptManager control.

Timer

The Timer control enables you to perform a synchronous or asynchronous postback at a defined interval. This is not a typical ASP.NET postback, but rather the XmlHttpRequest object that is generated in client-side script that is issuing a postback without refreshing the page. You can use the Timer control to perform periodic updates to your page with no user interaction. For example, if your web page is displaying stock prices, you might want to automatically refresh the stocks every minute so that it always shows the latest stock price (within a minute). No matter what the scenario, the Timer control typically is used together with an UpdatePanel to update a specific entity on the page.

UpdatePanel

The UpdatePanel control allows you to define a specific region on your page that can be updated asynchronously. UpdatePanel controls are one of the key controls of ASP.NET AJAX. They are used with the ScriptManager to enable partial-page rendering in your pages.

UpdateProgress

The UpdateProgress control enables you to provide visual feedback to your users while an asynchronous process is running. This control is important because it allows you to give your users visual cues that something is happening in the background while they are using your system.

The Visual Studio controls will be covered in greater detail in Chapter 3, "The ScriptManager and ScriptManagerProxy Controls."

Introducing the Visual Studio Projects and Web Site Items

Visual Studio 2008 provides a number of project and web site item templates to ease the process of AJAX-enabled projects and project items. This section explains each of these items.

Projects

There are several project templates that are available to you as a developer using Visual Studio 2008. These templates can save you a lot of time and effort when trying to develop a specific type of ASP.NET AJAX-based solutions (see Figure 2.2).

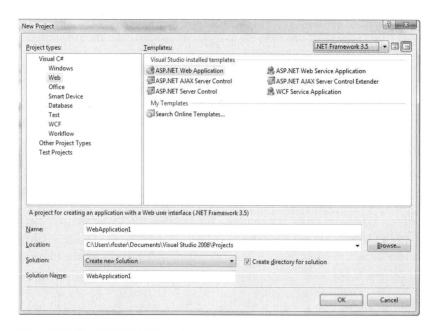

FIGURE 2.2   ASP.NET AJAX projects.

ASP.NET AJAX Server Control

ASP.NET AJAX Server Control projects are used to create AJAX-enabled server controls that you can distribute to your development teams and different server environments. An example of an AJAX Server Control is an autocomplete textbox that does asynchronous lookups to a web service as text in the textbox changes (or as you type).

ASP.NET AJAX Server Control Extender

ASP.NET AJAX Server Control Extenders enable you to wrap a non-AJAX server control and add AJAX functionality (or "extend" it). It is intuitive to use an AJAX Server Control Extender when you need to add similar AJAX functionality to multiple server controls, rather than creating separate controls to provide this similar functionality. An example of an AJAX Server Control Extender would be a control that does an asynchronous lookup to a web service based on a particular control that you hover over. Figure 2.3 illustrates the functionality of NetFlix.com when you hover over a movie; it does an asynchronous lookup to show you information about the movie.

FIGURE 2.3   NetFlix.com asynchronous lookup.

Web Site Items

There are three categories of web site items that you can add to your project: client-side items, page items, and services. Figure 2.4 shows the web site items (circled) that can be added to your project.

The AJAX Client Behavior, AJAX Client Control, and AJAX Client Library web site items are simply JavaScript templates you can use as a starting point to create each type of object. These templates are important because they provide a base framework for each item to interact with the ScriptManager object, which can save you a little bit of coding each time you implement one of these templates.

The page items, AJAX Master Page and AJAX Web Form, are essentially a regular master page and web form with a ScriptManager object added. Because the ScriptManager object is required for each page that uses ASP.NET AJAX, you can save some time by utilizing these templates.

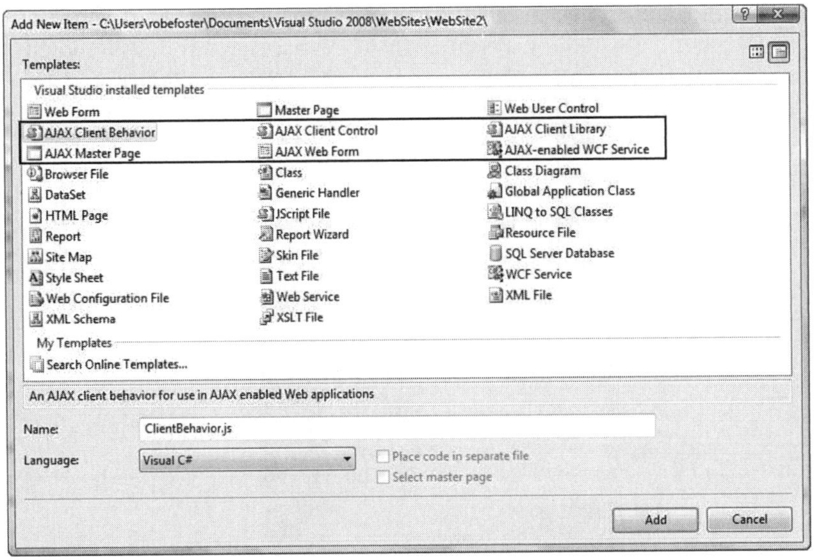

FIGURE 2.4   Web site items.

There is only one item in the Services category of web site items, and it is an important one: AJAX-enabled WCF Service. This is a template you can use to quickly create a WCF-based web service that can be registered with a ScriptManager control on your page.

Introducing the AJAX Control Toolkit

You can't mention ASP.NET AJAX without including the AJAX Control Toolkit. This is something that is *not* included with Visual Studio 2008 because it is a community-based project on CodePlex. This means that anyone in the community (as well as the ASP.NET product team) can contribute code and/or controls to the project. You can download the AJAX Control Toolkit at http://www.codeplex.com/AtlasControlToolkit.

As you dive deeper into ASP.NET AJAX, you will find that the AJAX Control Toolkit is arguably one of the most valuable aspects of ASP.NET AJAX itself as the controls are usable in the real-world *and* they contain a lot of useful code (you can download the source as well) that you can use as a learning tool or as a base for creating your own control. The following list shows controls that currently are available:

Accordion	DropDown	NoBot	Slider
AlwaysVisibleControl	DropShadow	NumericUpDown	SlideShow
Animation	DynamicPopulate	PagingBulleted-List	Tabs
AutoComplete	FilteredTextBox	Password-Strength	TextBoxWatermark
Calendar	HoverMenu	PopupControl	ToggleButton
CascadingDropDown	ListSearch	Rating	UpdatePanel-Animation
CollapsiblePanel	MaskedEdit	ReorderList	ValidatorCallout
ConfirmButton	ModalPopup	ResizableControl	
DragPanel	MutuallyExclusive-Checkbox		RoundedCorners

You learn more about the AJAX Control Toolkit in Chapter 6, "Using the ASP.NET AJAX Control Toolkit."

Summary

ASP.NET AJAX has tremendous value to you as an ASP.NET developer. You can easily provide your users with a rich user experience without having to change the many patterns and best practices that you have already learned in ASP.NET. Although this chapter was just an introduction to each of the options available to you in ASP.NET AJAX, Visual Studio 2008, and the .NET Framework 3.5, it is important that you know what tools are available to you before deep-diving into each option.

In the next few chapters, you will learn about each option in detail so that you can begin building effective ASP.NET AJAX-based applications.

PART II

Working with ASP.NET 3.5 AJAX

IN THIS PART

CHAPTER 3

The ScriptManager and ScriptManagerProxy Controls

The ScriptManager control is the heart of ASP.NET AJAX. It is responsible for managing and generating AJAX-enabled scripts and functionality for your web pages. In this section, you learn about the functionality of the ScriptManager control and how you can use it in your ASP.NET AJAX-enabled applications.

About the ScriptManager Control

The ScriptManager control provides a lot of functionality to your pages. If you have ever seen a demonstration of ScriptManager and ASP.NET AJAX, then it is likely you have seen how ScriptManager works together with the UpdatePanel to enable partial-page rendering of a web page. This is where the PostBack, which is associated with a typical out-of-the box ASP.NET web application, is suppressed; only a piece of the page updates either by a user action or by using the ASP.NET AJAX timer control. (You learn about partial-page rendering later in this chapter.) Although partial-page rendering is an important part of ASP.NET AJAX, the ScriptManager control provides a lot more functionality; it is important that you have a deep knowledge of this object.

Before you can use the ScriptManager, you must either drag an instance of it onto your page from the Visual Studio Toolbox or create a new AJAX Web Form by adding a new item to your web project. Figure 3.1 shows the AJAX Extensions section of the Visual Studio 2008 Toolbox.

FIGURE 3.1   Visual Studio 2008 Toolbox: ASP.NET Extensions.

If you are creating a new page and would like to use ASP.NET AJAX, you should add an AJAX Web Form to your project, as illustrated in Figure 3.2.

Creating an AJAX Web Form in your project gives you a preconfigured web page that can take advantage of ASP.NET AJAX. Listing 3.1 is an example of the template that gets created when you add an AJAX Web Form to your ASP.NET web project.

LISTING 3.1   ASP.NET AJAX Web Form Template

```
<%@ Page Language="C#" %>


<!DOCTYPE html PUBLIC "-//W3C//DTD XHTML 1.0
Transitional//EN" "http://www.w3.org/TR/xhtml1/DTD/xhtml1-transitional.dtd">

<%@ Page Language="C#" %>

<!DOCTYPE html PUBLIC "-//W3C//DTD XHTML 1.0 Transitional//EN"
"http://www.w3.org/TR/xhtml1/DTD/xhtml1-transitional.dtd">

<script runat="server">
```

```
</script>

<html xmlns="http://www.w3.org/1999/xhtml">
<head runat="server">
    <title>Untitled Page</title>
    <script type="text/javascript">

    function pageLoad() {
    }

    </script>
</head>
<body>
    <form id="form1" runat="server">
    <div>
        <asp:ScriptManager ID="ScriptManager1" runat="server" />
    </div>
    </form>
</body>
</html>
```

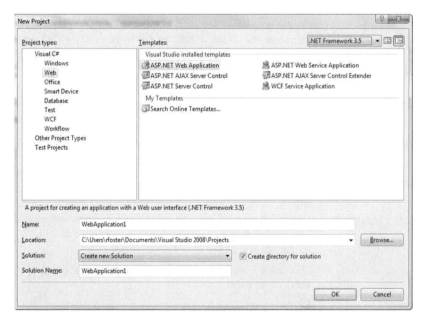

FIGURE 3.2   Add an AJAX Web Form to your project.

The difference between an AJAX Web Form and an ASP.NET Web Form is that the AJAX Web Form contains a JavaScript section with a single function called pageLoad and a

ScriptManager control. Although this functionality can be replicated easily with an ASP.NET Web Form, your code will have a more consistent look if you use AJAX Web Forms.

Because a page can have one and only one ScriptManager control, the ScriptManagerProxy control allows you to reference a ScriptManager control that has been defined on an inherited ASP.NET master page. This is important because you can simply drop a ScriptManager control onto your master page, and all pages that inherit that master page will be able to use it by referencing it with the ScriptManager Proxy control.

ScriptManager Properties, Methods, and Events

Understanding the ScriptManager control means knowing about each property, method, and event that it exposes. In this section, you learn about these properties, methods, and events. Table 3.1 describes the ScriptManager control properties.

Properties

TABLE 3.1   ScriptManager Control Properties

Property	Description
AllowCustomErrorsRedirect	If true, redirects to page defined in the CustomErrors section of the Web.Config.
AsyncPostBackErrorMessage	Custom message text that can be sent during an asynchronous postback error. If blank, the exception message will be used. Can be set by code in the page's markup or handled by the AsyncPostbackError event.
AsyncPostBackTimeout	Number of seconds before the asynchronous call times out. If this property is 0, then it will not timeout.
AuthenticationService	Collection that stores the path to the page that handles page authentication.
EnablePageMethods	Enables you to call page-defined methods as web services.
EnablePartialPageRendering	Enables you to use partial-page rendering with an UpdatePanel control.
EnableScriptGlobalization	Enables the ScriptManager to add globalization information to the client-side script that is generated and pushed to the page.
EnableScriptLocalization	Enables the ScriptManager control to generate localized versions of scripts.
EnableViewState	Enables ViewState for the ScriptManager control.
LoadScriptsBeforeUI	Renders the scripts before rendering the HTML output in the browser.
ProfileService	Collection of items that enable access to a profile web service.
RoleService	Collection of items that enable client-side authentication.

TABLE 3.1   Continued

Property	Description
ScriptMode	Tells the ScriptManager what type of scripts to load if more than one type is available. Valid values are Auto, Inherit, Debug, and Release.
ScriptPath	A path that can be specified to load scripts instead of from the ASP.NET AJAX assembly web resources.
Scripts	A collection of scripts that the ScriptManager should include in the page.
Services	A collection of web services references that the ScriptManager should include in the page.

Methods

NOTE

Note that ScriptManager has a lot of methods, most of which are inherited from the Control class. Table 3.2 describes all the local methods (not inherited) of the ScriptManager object. Note that all methods marked with an asterisk (*) are static methods.

TABLE 3.2   ScriptManager Control Methods

Method	Description
ScriptManager	Constructor.
LoadPostData	Loads data from the post to determine the source for the asynchronous call.
OnAsyncPostBackError	Raises the AsynchPostBackError event.
OnResolveScriptReference	Raises the ResolveScriptMethod for each Scripts property collection.
*RegisterArrayDeclaration	Registers a JavaScript array with the ScriptManager control and adds the array to the page's script output.
*RegisterClientScriptBlock	Registers a JavaScript script block with the ScriptManager control and adds the script block to the page's script output.
*RegisterClientScriptInclude	Registers a client script with the ScriptManager control and adds the client script reference to the page's script output.
*RegisterClientScriptResource	Registers a client script that is embedded in an assembly.

TABLE 3.2   Continued

Method	Description
RegisterDataItem	Enables you to send data to a control during partial-page rendering.
RegisterDispose	Registers a dispose script for a control that is running inside an UpdatePanel control.
*RegisterExpandAttribute	Registers a custom attribute (name/value pair) of a specified control with the ScriptManager.
RegisterExtenderControl	Registers an extender control with the ScriptManager.
*RegisterHiddenField	Registers a hidden field that is running inside an UpdatePanel control.
*RegisterOnSubmitStatement	Registers JavaScript that will execute every time that a page posts back.
RegisterPostbackControl	Registers a control that is running inside an UpdatePanel control that will be used to postback the UpdatePanel.
RegisterScriptControl	Registers a Script control with the ScriptManager control.
*RegisterStartupScript	Registers a startup script that will be executed when a page postback occurs.
Render	Renders the ScriptManager control's output to the browser window. Note that this is an overridden method from the Control class.

Table 3.3 shows the events that are exposed from the ScriptManager control.

Events

TABLE 3.3   ScriptManager Control Events

Event	Description
AsyncPostbackError	Raised when an error is thrown during an asynchronous post-back.
ResolveScriptReference	Raised when a script is registered in the scripts collection of the ScriptManager control.

In the next few sections, you learn about the four pieces of functionality that are exposed by the ScriptManager control:

▶ JavaScript proxy classes for web services

▶ Client-Script functionality

▶ Authentication and profile application services

▶ Partial-page rendering

JavaScript Proxy Classes for Web Services

One of the most useful (not to mention time saving) features of the ScriptManager control is its ability to generate JavaScript proxy classes for calling web services. This can be very advantageous to you as a developer because you will have much less code that you have to manually write and maintain just to make an asynchronous server-side call to a web service.

Before you can use AJAX to asynchronously call a web service, you need to create a web service to call. To keep things simple, in this example (largely so that you can focus on the AJAX and not the web service itself), you use AJAX and the ScriptManager to call a WCF-based web service that simply adds two numbers together and returns a result. This will simulate a server-side web service call, process the call, and return the result to the client, asynchronously. You can add an AJAX-enabled WCF service to your project by right clicking your project in the Solution Explorer and then clicking the Add New Item menu.

The WCF web service is defined by two files: MyMathService.svc and MyMathService.cs, shown in Listings 3.2 and 3.3.

LISTING 3.2   MyMathService.svc

```
<%@ ServiceHost Language="C#" Debug="true" Service="MyMathService"
CodeBehind="~/App_Code/MyMathService.cs" %>
```

MyMathService.svc is a file that provides a public interface into your WCF-based Web service. Although this can be done any number of ways, this example hosts the web service in the context of IIS.

LISTING 3.3   MyMathService.cs

```
using System;
using System.Linq;
using System.Runtime.Serialization;
using System.ServiceModel;
using System.ServiceModel.Activation;
using System.ServiceModel.Web;

[ServiceContract(Namespace = "")]
[AspNetCompatibilityRequirements(RequirementsMode =
AspNetCompatibilityRequirementsMode.Allowed)]
public class MyMathServicesvc
{

        // Add [WebGet] attribute to use HTTP GET
        [OperationContract]
    public int AddNumbers(int x, int y)
```

LISTING 3.3   Continued

```
    {
        return x + y;
    }


        // Add more operations here and mark them with [OperationContract]
}
```

For this example, the code in the MyMathService.cs file is very simple. There is one function called AddNumbers that accepts two integers. It adds the two numbers that are passed into the function and returns the sum of the two numbers.

> **NOTE**
>
> Note that this sample web service is designed with simplicity in mind so that you can focus on the functionality of the ScriptManager control instead of the inner workings of WCF. A more advanced example will be covered in the next example to demonstrate the JavaScript Object Notation (JSON) capabilities of ASP.NET AJAX.

Now that you understand the web service that will be consumed by an ASP.NET AJAX-enabled page, you are ready to learn how to consume it with the ASP.NET AJAX ScriptManager control. Listing 3.4 displays the AJAXWebServiceProxy.aspx web page, which consumes a web service by using the ScriptManager control.

LISTING 3.4   AJAXWebServiceProxy.aspx

```
<%@ Page Language="C#" %>


<!DOCTYPE html PUBLIC "-//W3C//DTD XHTML 1.0 Transitional//EN"
"http://www.w3.org/TR/xhtml1/DTD/xhtml1-transitional.dtd">


<script runat="server">

</script>

<html xmlns="http://www.w3.org/1999/xhtml">
<head id="Head1" runat="server">
    <title>Add Numbers</title>
    <script type="text/javascript">

    function pageLoad() {
    }
```

```
        function OnSucceeded(result){
          //display result in div
          divResult.innerHTML = result;
        }
        function onButtonClick(){
           var p = new tempuri.org.MyMathService();
           p.AddNumbers(txtNum1.value, txtNum2.value, OnSucceeded);
        }
    </script>
</head>
<body>
    <form id="form1" runat="server">
    <div>
        <asp:ScriptManager ID="MyScriptManager" runat="server" >
            <Services>
                <asp:ServiceReference Path="~/MyMathService.svc" />
            </Services>
        </asp:ScriptManager>
    </div>
    </form>
    <table>
        <tr>
            <td>Number 1:</td>
            <td><input type=text id=txtNum1 /></td>
        </tr>
        <tr>
            <td>Number 2:</td>
            <td><input type=text id=txtNum2 /></td>
        </tr>
        <tr>
            <td>Result:</td>
            <td><div id=divResult></div></td>
        </tr>
        <tr>
            <td></td>
            <td><input type=button id=btn value="Add Nums"
onclick="onButtonClick();" /></td>
        </tr>
    </table>

</body>
</html>
```

Figure 3.3 illustrates the page that is rendered by the code in Listing 3.4.

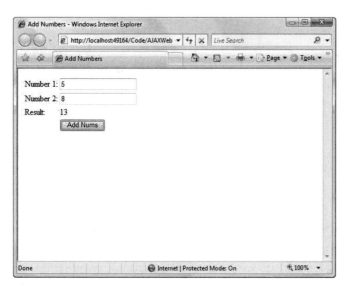

FIGURE 3.3   Web service proxies.

Now that you have seen the code and the rendered page, it is time to dig into the code behind the scenes that makes this happen. In Listing 3.4, first take note of the ScriptManager control. Notice the following block of code:

```
<asp:ScriptManager ID="MyScriptManager" runat="server" >
    <Services>
        <asp:ServiceReference Path="~/MyMathService.svc" />
    </Services>
</asp:ScriptManager>
```

The ScriptManager control (named MyScriptManager) has a Services element inside it, which defines a service—actually, it's the WCF-based web service defined in Listing 3.2. This is important to note as this small amount of code tells the ScriptManager to generate a JavaScript proxy you can use to call the web service. In the past, you would have had to write (and maintain) many lines of code to accomplish the same task.

Next, take note of the two JavaScript functions that are defined in the page: OnButtonClick and OnSucceeded. First, OnButtonClick is invoked when a user clicks on the Add Nums button. When a user clicks on the button and the OnButtonClick method is fired, an instance of the web service is created and the AddNumbers function can then be called from JavaScript.

NOTE

Actually coding this type of functionality is made easier by use of the Visual Studio 2008 JavaScript IntelliSense and debugging features.

When you make a call to the AddNumbers web service, you must remember that this will be an asynchronous call. That is why that you must also pass a callback function into the AddNumbers function. Additionally, you have the option to pass in a failed callback function for when the asynchronous call fails for some reason and also a user context object for the user's credentials. After the OnSucceeded function fires (this will happen *very* quickly as there is minimal web service processing), the result of the web service call is loaded into the results div tag to display the results to the user.

In its simplest form, it is literally that easy to asynchronously call web services using ASP.NET AJAX. In this example, however, notice that the web service was passing back a primitive integer data type. In the real world, this is not often the case because your web services will typically return a typed object. How do you think that the ScriptManager control will react to a typed object that is returned from a web service? Lucky for the ASP.NET AJAX community, it *will* allow this type of functionality via the JSON serializer.

JSON is required when you are returning typed objects from your web service to client-side code. Traditionally in AJAX, this would be a JSON string that would be returned from a web service as a string and evaluated on the client-side. In ASP.NET AJAX, much of this functionality is handled automatically, and you can simply receive the object as a result of the callback and immediately begin to call its properties as a typed JavaScript object.

Listing 3.5 is a simple example of a WCF web service that returns employee information as a typed object. Again, not to get bogged down in the complexities of WCF, this is a very simple example.

LISTING 3.5   Get Employee Information WCF Service

```
using System;
using System.Linq;
using System.Runtime.Serialization;
using System.ServiceModel;
using System.ServiceModel.Activation;
using System.ServiceModel.Web;


[ServiceContract(Namespace = "")]
[AspNetCompatibilityRequirements(RequirementsMode =
AspNetCompatibilityRequirementsMode.Allowed)]
public class MyMathServicesvc
{
    // Add [WebGet] attribute to use HTTP GET
    [OperationContract]
    public int AddNumbers(int x, int y)
    {
        return x + y;
    }
```

LISTING 3.5   Continued

```
    // Add more operations here and mark them with
    [OperationContract]
}

[ServiceContract]
[AspNetCompatibilityRequirements(RequirementsMode =
AspNetCompatibilityRequirementsMode.Allowed)]
public class MyEmployeeService
{

    [OperationContract]
    public Employee GetEmployeeByID(int EmpID)
    {
        return new Employee(1234);
    }

}

[DataContract]
public class Employee
{
    private string _firstName = "na";
    private string _lastName;

    public string FirstName
    {
        get { return this._firstName; }
    }

    public string LastName
    {
        get { return this._lastName; }
    }

    public Employee(int empID)
    {
        if (empID == 1234)
        {
            _firstName = "Rob";
            _lastName = "Foster";
        }
        else
        {
            _firstName = "NOT FOUND";
```

```
        _lastName = "NOT FOUND";
      }
    }
}
```

This code can be invoked and handled with the following two JavaScript functions, which invoke the web service and load the results of the web service (an employee's first name and last name) into two div tags on the page.

```
function onGetEmployeeClick(){
    var p = new tempuri.org.MyEmployeeService();
    p.GetEmployeeByID(1234, onGetEmployeeCallback);
}

function onGetEmployeeCallback(result){
    var emp = eval(Sys.Serialization.JavaScriptSerializer.deserialize(result));
    divFirstName.innerHTML = emp.FirstName;
    divLastName.innerHTML = emp.LastName;
}
```

Because the results returned into the callback function are JSON, you must deserialize them into an object that can be evaluated. You can do this by using the `Sys.Serialization.JavaScriptSerializer.deserialize` method, which will be covered in the "Sys.Serialization" section later in the next chapter.

As you can see from the examples in this section, it is very easy to asynchronously call web services from client script with ASP.NET AJAX. In the next section, you learn about partial-page rendering.

Partial-Page Rendering

Partial-page rendering is another time-saving benefit of ASP.NET AJAX. It is accomplished by using a combination of the ScriptManager control, an UpdatePanel control, and traditional ASP.NET controls. You learn more about the UpdatePanel control in the next chapter, but you must have some familiarity with it before learning the capabilities of ASP.NET AJAX's client-script functionality.

You can use partial-page rendering to AJAX-enable a section of your page at a time. For example, you might have a login control on your page, as well as some other sections that perform data retrievals against a database. In this instance, you can easily place each distinct unit of functionality (the login control and the data retrieval items) into its own update panel, which will allow each part of the page to make independent asynchronous calls.

Again, you learn more about the UpdatePanel control in the next chapter, but you must get a basic understanding of how the code looks as this example will be expanded when discussing the client-script functionality of ASP.NET AJAX. Figure 3.4 illustrates the page that you will be learning how to build.

When the user clicks the Button control, the page is executing a query against the Northwind sample database and displaying the results in a GridView control, as you can see in Figure 3.4. The query that is being executed is shown in Listing 3.6.

Note that you can download the Northwind sample SQL Server database from the following URL: http://www.microsoft.com/downloads/details.aspx?FamilyID=06616212-0356-46A0-8DA2-EEBC53A68034&displaylang=en.

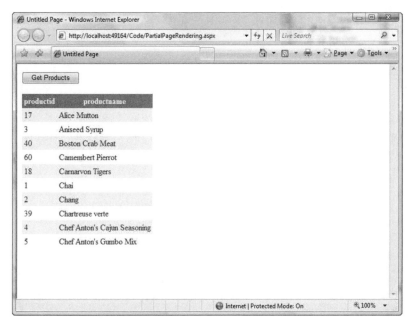

FIGURE 3.4   Partial-page rendering.

LISTING 3.6   Products_sel Stored Procedure

```
CREATE PROCEDURE products_sel

AS

SELECT TOP 10
    productid
    , productname
FROM Products
```

Listing 3.7 describes the ASP.NET code behind the web page. Note that you will need to update the connection string to reflect your installation of the Northwind database.

LISTING 3.7   PartialPageRendering.aspx

```
<%@ Page Language="C#" %>
<%@ Import Namespace="System.Data.SqlClient" %>
<!DOCTYPE html PUBLIC "-//W3C//DTD XHTML 1.0 Transitional//EN"
"http://www.w3.org/TR/xhtml1/DTD/xhtml1-transitional.dtd">

<script runat="server">

    protected void btnGetProducts_Click(object sender, EventArgs e)
    {
        SqlConnection cn = new SqlConnection(
"Data Source=localhost;Initial Catalog=Northwind;User ID=sa;Password=password;");
        SqlCommand cmd = new SqlCommand("products_sel", cn);
        cmd.CommandType = System.Data.CommandType.StoredProcedure;
        try
        {
            cn.Open();
            gvProducts.DataSource = cmd.ExecuteReader();
            gvProducts.DataBind();

        }
        finally
        {
            cn.Close();
            cmd.Dispose();
            cn.Dispose();
        }
    }

    protected void Page_Load(object sender, EventArgs e)
    {

    }
</script>

<html xmlns="http://www.w3.org/1999/xhtml">
<head runat="server">
    <title>Untitled Page</title>
    <script type="text/javascript">

      function pageLoad() {
      }

    </script>
```

3

LISTING 3.7   Continued

```
</head>
<body>
    <form id="form1" runat="server">
    <div>
        <asp:ScriptManager ID="ScriptManager1" runat="server" />
        <asp:UpdatePanel ID="UpdatePanel1" runat="server">
            <contenttemplate>
                <asp:Button ID="btnGetProducts" runat="server"
Text="Get Products" OnClick="btnGetProducts_Click" />
                <br />
                <br />
                <asp:GridView ID="gvProducts" runat="server"
CellPadding="4" ForeColor="#333333" GridLines="None">
                    <footerstyle backcolor="#507CD1" font-bold="True"
➥forecolor="White" />
                    <rowstyle backcolor="#EFF3FB" />
                    <pagerstyle backcolor="#2461BF"
➥forecolor="White" horizontalalign="Center" />
                    <selectedrowstyle backcolor="#D1DDF1"
➥font-bold="True" forecolor="#333333" />
                    <headerstyle backcolor="#507CD1" font-bold="True"
➥forecolor="White" />
                    <editrowstyle backcolor="#2461BF" />
                    <alternatingrowstyle backcolor="White" />
                </asp:GridView>
                <br />
            </contenttemplate>
        </asp:UpdatePanel>
    </div>
    </form>
</body>
</html>
```

If you look closely at the code, you will notice that it's not much different from any traditional ASP.NET page, with the following exceptions:

1. There is a ScriptManager control on the page.

2. The ASP.NET Button and GridView controls are actually contained within an UpdatePanel control.

Because of conditions 1 and 2, the postback is suppressed and the page will not flicker when the button is clicked. Isn't that easy? Even though Listing 3.7 is just an introduction to the UpdatePanel control, you can already see the power and flexibility that it provides to you as an ASP.NET developer.

In the next section, you learn about the very extensive ASP.NET AJAX client-side JavaScript libraries available to you.

Summary

Having a solid foundation in the ScriptManager will make your ASP.NET AJAX programming experience much more enjoyable. In this chapter, you have learned about the benefits of using the ScriptManager control by looking at real-world examples of how to use it.

TABLE 4.1   ASP.NET AJAX Client-Side Namespaces

Namespace	Description
{Global}	Contains all shared members and types utilized by and available to all objects in the object model, including `Array`, `Boolean`, `Error`, `Number`, `Object`, and `String`
Sys	Contains all of the primary classes and base JavaScript classes of the object model; it is a root namespace of the client-side object model
Sys.Net	Communicates between client-side JavaScript and server-side web services
Sys.Serialization	Serializes objects with client-side code
Sys.Services	Contains all types and members that are used to reference the ASP.NET profile service, authentication service, and other application-layer services
Sys.UI	Contains types related to user interface objects
Sys.WebForms	Renders partial pages with ASP.NET AJAX

First and foremost, you should take note of the JavaScript base type extensions. There are definitions for the following objects:

▶ `Array`

▶ `Boolean`

▶ `Date`

▶ `Error`

▶ `Number`

▶ `Object`

▶ `String`

It is likely that you could already have definitions for these objects in your own custom JavaScript libraries; however, they are now part of the ASP.NET AJAX client-side object model.

The `global` namespace also has a number of shortcut functions that you can use to quickly perform tasks, which are described in Table 4.2.

TABLE 4.2   Global Namespace Shortcut Functions

Function	Description
$addHandler	Adds a handler to a DOM element by specifying the element, the event that you want to attach to, and a function to call when the event is raised
$addHandlers	Allows you to add a list of handlers to a DOM element
$clearHandlers	Clears all handlers for a specified DOM element
$create	Creates, initializes, and registers a client-side component with ASP.NET AJAX
$find	Finds a registered component on the page and returns a reference to that component; you can also specify the Parent component if it is nested inside of an element such as a DIV or a SPAN
$get	Returns either a reference to a control or an array of all components that have been registered with the ASP.NET AJAX client library
$removeHandler	Removes a DOM event handler from a DOM element

Listing 4.1 illustrates two JavaScript functions that are defined in the global namespace.

LISTING 4.1   Global JavaScript Functions

```
<script type="text/javascript">

  function pageLoad() {
        $addHandler($get("btnGetProducts"), "click", processClientClick);
  }
  function processClientClick(){
        $get("Label1").innerHTML = "Data Retrieved!";
  }
</script>
```

In the pageLoad function, a handler is added to the click event of a Button control named btnGetProducts. When the button is clicked, the processClientClick handler is fired, which updates a Label control on the page (note that ASP.NET Label controls get rendered as DIVs).

NOTE

In traditional ASP.NET, it is very easy to add client-side handlers to server-side controls. It should be noted that it is much trickier to dynamically attach events with JavaScript to ASP.NET controls that have been rendered to the browser. The previous example illustrates how simple this process is now with the ASP.NET AJAX client library.

Sys

The Sys namespace is the root namespace of the ASP.NET AJAX client-side library. It contains classes and interfaces that are core to the ASP.NET AJAX client-side object model. The Sys namespace contains many classes that you need to be familiar with, beginning with the Application class.

The Application class exposes a few events that you need to interact with when you are doing advanced ASP.NET AJAX development. Table 4.3 describes these events.

TABLE 4.3   Events of the Application Class

Event	Description
Init	Initialize event that gets raised after all of the ScriptManager control's scripts have been loaded, but before any objects are created
load	Load event that gets raised after the init event and after all ASP.NET AJAX-aware components have been created and initialized
unload	Unload event that is raised just before all ASP.NET AJAX-aware components are disposed

These events are essential for you to understand as you will likely have to do some pre- and postprocessing of components and data in ASP.NET AJAX.

You can add and remove handlers to these events by calling their respective add and remove methods on the Sys.Application class, as illustrated by the following code example:

```
function pageLoad() {
    Sys.Application.add_init(app_init);
    Sys.Application.add_load(app_load);
    Sys.Application.add_unload(app_unload);
}

function app_init(){
  //initialize logic here
}

function app_load(){
  //load logic here
}

function app_unload(){
  //unload logic here
}
```

Another class that you should be familiar with in the Sys namespace is the Debug class. This class provides you with a handy way to log to the Visual Studio 2008 debugger trace as well as perform assertions in your JavaScript code. Table 4.4 describes the methods that are exposed by the debugger class.

TABLE 4.4   Methods of the Debugger Class

Method	Description
assert	Executes an assert condition in your client-side code; if the condition evaluates to false, a message is displayed to you and you are prompted to enter break mode
clearTrace	Clears all trace messages in the trace console
Fail	Forces the running code into break mode
trace	Appends a line of text to the Visual Studio 2008 debugger trace window
traceDump	Dumps an object to the Visual Studio debugger trace window

Sys.Net

The Sys.Net namespace contains classes that help you perform your asynchronous service calls. Though it appears that most of the process is automated when you drop a ScriptManager control onto your page, a thorough understanding of the classes contained in this namespace can save you some debugging time in the future.

The Sys.Net namespace contains the classes described in Table 4.5 (note that there are more, but these are the most used).

TABLE 4.5   Common Classes of the Sys.Net Namespace

Class	Description
WebServiceProxy	Enables you to invoke a method on a web service that is registered in the <Scripts> section of the ScriptManager control. Though the proxy itself is automatically generated, the WebServiceProxy class provides the functionality to invoke the registered service.
WebRequest	Allows you to make client-side web requests. This object will be used if you are performing something other than a simple web service call. For example, you will use this if you are calling a web service that implements the REST pattern.
WebRequestManager	Helps you to manage each request that is made to a web service.
WebServiceError	This is the object that is returned when a web service throws an exception back to the client.
XMLHttpExecutor	Allows you to manually make asynchronous calls using the browser's XMLHTTP object.

LISTING 4.2   Continued

```csharp
    private string _firstName;
    private string _lastName;

    public int ID
    {
        get { return _Id; }
        set { _Id = value; }
    }

    public string FirstName
    {
        get { return _firstName; }
        set { _firstName = value; }
    }

    public string LastName
    {
        get { return _lastName; }
        set { _lastName = value; }
    }
}
```

You can easily create a server-side instance of this class with C# using the following code excerpt:

```csharp
Employee emp = new Employee();
emp.ID = 1234;
emp.FirstName = "Rob";
emp.LastName = "Foster";
```

Now, if you want to serialize this object using JSON, you need to serialize the instance of this class into a specific format that can be interpreted by JavaScript. The syntax for this class would look like the following code excerpt:

```json
{
"ID":1234,
"FirstName":"Rob",
"LastName":"Foster"
}
```

You can write all of the plumbing code that is required to properly serialize and deserialize JSON objects; however, the ASP.NET 3.5 object model provides all of the necessary objects that you can use to accomplish this out of the box.

On the server side, these classes are located in the System.Web.Script.Serialization namespace. Specifically, you need to use the JavaScriptSerializer class, which allows you to easily serialize and deserialize a server-side class instance into JSON for client-side processing.

On the client side, you can use the Sys.Serialization namespace to serialize and deserialize JSON objects for processing with JavaScript. Like System.Web.Script.Serialization, the Sys.Serialization namespace contains a JavaScriptSerializer class.

Table 4.6 describes how the server-side (or managed) data types of your classes will be represented in client-side JavaScript when they are serialized.

TABLE 4.6   Serialization Data Type Conversions

Server-Side Data Type	Client-Side Data Type
String	String
Null values (null, DBNull, \0, etc.)	Null
Numeric data types (all)	Number
DateTime	Date object
Enumerations	Integer value of the enumeration
Array, ArrayList, List, etc.	JavaScript array with JSON syntax
GUID	String

The benefits of using the JavaScriptSerializer classes (server- and client-side) is that the serialization code has been written for you and they are flexible enough that you can easily serialize and deserialize most managed objects.

Listing 4.3 is an example of an application that serializes a server-side instance of the Employee class (Listing 4.2) and then processes the JSON instance of the object using JavaScript.

LISTING 4.3   Using Sys.Serialization to Process a JSON Object

```
<%@ Page Language="C#" %>
<%@ Import Namespace="System.Web.Script.Serialization" %>
<!DOCTYPE html PUBLIC "-//W3C//DTD XHTML 1.0 Transitional//EN"
 "http://www.w3.org/TR/xhtml1/DTD/xhtml1-transitional.dtd">

<script runat="server">

    protected void Page_Load(object sender, EventArgs e)
    {
```

LISTING 4.3   Continued

```
    }

    protected void cmdSerializeClass_Click(object sender, EventArgs e)
    {
        Employee emp = new Employee();
        emp.ID = int.Parse(txtID.Text.Trim());
        emp.FirstName = txtFirstName.Text.Trim();
        emp.LastName = txtLastName.Text.Trim();
        JavaScriptSerializer jsSerializer = new JavaScriptSerializer();
        StringBuilder sb = new StringBuilder();
        jsSerializer.Serialize(emp, sb);
        lblSerialized.Text = sb.ToString();

    }

</script>

<html xmlns="http://www.w3.org/1999/xhtml">
<head runat="server">
    <title>Untitled Page</title>
    <script type="text/javascript">

      function pageLoad() {
      }

      function getSerializedEmployee(){
         var emp = Sys.Serialization.JavaScriptSerializer.deserialize(
<%=lblSerialized.ClientID %>.innerText);
         document.getElementById('txtClientID').value = emp.ID;
         document.getElementById('txtClientFirstName').value = emp.FirstName;
         document.getElementById('txtClientLastName').value = emp.LastName;
      }

      function saveEmployee(){
         var emp = Sys.Serialization.JavaScriptSerializer.deserialize(
<%=lblSerialized.ClientID %>.innerText);
         emp.ID = document.getElementById('txtClientID').value
         emp.FirstName = document.getElementById('txtClientFirstName').value
         emp.LastName = document.getElementById('txtClientLastName').value

         <%=lblSerialized.ClientID %>.innerText =
 Sys.Serialization.JavaScriptSerializer.serialize(emp);
      }

    </script>
```

```
</head>
<body>
    <form id="form1" runat="server">
    <div>
        <asp:ScriptManager ID="ScriptManager1" runat="server" />

    </div>
    <table>
        <tr>
            <td colspan="2"><h2>Server-Side</h2></td>
        </tr>
        <tr>
            <td>ID:</td>
            <td>
                <asp:TextBox ID="txtID" runat="server"></asp:TextBox>
            </td>
        </tr>
        <tr>
            <td>First Name:</td>
            <td>
                <asp:TextBox ID="txtFirstName" runat="server"></asp:TextBox>
            </td>
        </tr>
        <tr>
            <td>Last Name:</td>
            <td>
                <asp:TextBox ID="txtLastName" runat="server"></asp:TextBox>
            </td>
        </tr>
        <tr>
            <td></td>
            <td>
                <asp:Button ID="cmdSerializeClass" runat="server"
Text="Serialize Class" onclick="cmdSerializeClass_Click" /></td>
        </tr>
        <tr>
            <td>Serialized Class Instance: </td>
            <td><asp:Label ID="lblSerialized" runat="server" Text="">
</asp:Label></td>
        </tr>
    </table>

    <br />
    <hr />
    <br />
    <table>
```

Sys.Services

The `Sys.Services` namespace is used to expose a client-side API to access the ASP.NET profile service, authentication service, and other services. Traditionally, this was only available by doing the login processing on the server, which typically requires a postback in ASP.NET. In the following example, the `Sys.Services` client-side API is used to log a user in to an ASP.NET web site using Forms authentication.

First, Forms authentication has been enabled and two users have been added to the web site using the ASP.NET Configuration page, as illustrated in Figure 4.3.

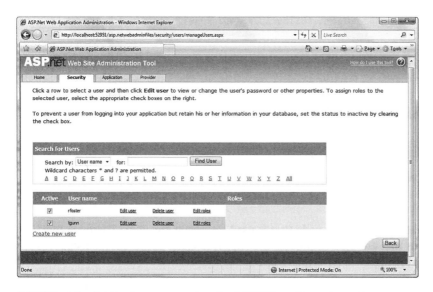

FIGURE 4.3   Adding two users using the ASP.NET configuration utility.

After you have configured security, you must insert a few entries into the configuration section of your Web.Config file, as shown in the following code sample:

```
<connectionStrings>
  <remove name="LocalSqlServer"/>
  <add name="LocalSqlServer"
    connectionString="data source=.\SQLEXPRESS;Integrated Security=SSPI;
  AttachDBFilename=¦DataDirectory¦aspnetdb.mdf;
  User Instance=true" providerName="System.Data.SqlClient" />
</connectionStrings>
<system.web.extensions>
  <scripting>
    <webServices>
      <authenticationService enabled="true" />
    </webServices>
```

```
    </scripting>
  </system.web.extensions>
```

This ensures that the local database will be used to store and read the ASP.NET configuration database (note that this could also point to a real SQL Server, and probably will in your environment depending on your configuration). Additionally, you need to configure the authentication service to be enabled. This forces the ScriptManager control to generate a client proxy to log the user in and out of the system.

Listing 4.4 is an example of using the client-side API to log in and log out of an ASP.NET site using Forms authentication.

NOTE

Note that the ASP.NET Membership scheme is irrelevant as it is defined by the Web.Config file, so the concept is the same no matter which membership provider you are using.

LISTING 4.4   AJAX Authentication

```
<%@ Page Language="C#" %>

<!DOCTYPE html PUBLIC "-//W3C//DTD XHTML 1.0 Transitional//EN"
➥"http://www.w3.org/TR/xhtml1/DTD/xhtml1-transitional.dtd">

<script runat="server">

</script>

<html xmlns="http://www.w3.org/1999/xhtml">
<head runat="server">
    <title>Login Example</title>
    <script type="text/javascript">
        function pageLoad()
        {
        }

        function Login()
        {
            Sys.Services.AuthenticationService.set_
➥defaultLoginCompletedCallback(loginComplete);

            Sys.Services.AuthenticationService.set_
➥defaultLogoutCompletedCallback(logoutComplete);
```

LISTING 4.4   Continued

```
            Sys.Services.AuthenticationService.login
➥(document.getElementById('txtUserId').value,

            document.getElementById('txtPassword').value,
➥false,null,null,null,null,'User Context');
        }

        function Logout()
        {
            Sys.Services.AuthenticationService.logout(null,
                null, null, null);
        }

        function loginComplete(validCredentials, userContext, methodName)
        {

            // Clear the user password.
            document.getElementById('txtPassword').value = '';

            if (validCredentials == true)
            {
                document.getElementById('txtUserId').value = '';
                document.getElementById('tblLogin').style.visibility = 'hidden';
                document.getElementById('tblLogout').style.visibility = '';

            }
            else
            {
                alert('Invalid credentials!');
            }
        }

        function logoutComplete(result)
        {
            document.getElementById('tblLogin').style.visibility = '';
            document.getElementById('tblLogout').style.visibility = 'hidden';
        }

        if (typeof(Sys) !== 'undefined') Sys.Application.notifyScriptLoaded();

    </script>
</head>
<body>
    <form id="form1" runat="server">
    <div>
        <asp:ScriptManager ID="ScriptManager1" runat="server" >
```

```
                </asp:ScriptManager>
        </div>

        <table id="tblLogin">
            <tr>
                <td>User ID:</td>
                <td><input type="text" id="txtUserId" /></td>
            </tr>
            <tr>
                <td>Password:</td>
                <td><input type="password" id="txtPassword" /></td>
            </tr>
            <tr>
                <td></td>
                <td><input type="button" id="btnLogin" value="Login"
➥onclick="Login();" /></td>
            </tr>
        </table>
        <table id="tblLogout" style="visibility:hidden">
            <tr>
                <td><input type="button" value="Logout" id="btnLogout"
➥onclick="Logout();" /></td>
            </tr>
        </table>
        </form>
</body>
</html>
```

The concept of the page is simple: A login page is presented to the user that they can use to log in to the ASP.NET web site. With this in mind, you should focus on two main JavaScript functions: Login and Logout.

Beginning with the Login function, it first registers two handlers with the API, which will get fired when the login and logout processes are completed, respectively. After the handlers are registered, a call is made to the Sys.Services.AuthenticationService.login method and the user's credentials are passed into the method. This is how the user gets logged in to the system, and as you can see, the process is quite simple other than a few lines of setup code (setting up the handlers).

The Logout function makes a call to the Sys.Services.AuthenticationService.logout function and passes null values into the function parameters. This clears the login cookie that gets set during the login process and the user will be formally logged out of the system.

The authentication service is very powerful in that you can expose a lot of functionality (login and logout) to your users without having to do a postback just to log them in to your web site.

Sys.UI

The `Sys.UI` namespace contains types that are directly related to working with the web user interface with ASP.NET AJAX. It contains members that help you determine key codes, mouse coordinates, mouse buttons, behaviors, and events of the ASP.NET AJAX client object model. The objects in this namespace are largely used to help support the user's interaction with the web page, but it also contains classes that allow you to interact with individual controls on the page. Table 4.7 describes the classes that are contained within the `Sys.UI` namespace.

TABLE 4.7   Classes of the `Sys.UI` Namespace

Name	Type	Description
Behavior	Class	Represents a base class that is an ASP.NET AJAX behavior. You can use this class to extend the functionality of a control (or DOM element) on your page. You should not create an instance of this class, but rather derive a class from the Behavior base class.
Bounds	Class	Represents the x, y, width, and height properties of a document element. For example, you can call the Sys.UI.DomElement.getBounds() method to return an instance of the Bounds class for a DOM element.
Control	Class	Represents the base class for all ASP.NET AJAX controls.
DomElement	Class	Represents a DOM element on the page.
DomEvent	Class	Provides the functionality to create and attach an event to a DOM element.
Key	Enumeration	Represents a key code.
MouseButton	Enumeration	Represents mouse buttons (leftButton, middleButton, and rightButton).
Point	Class	Represents the x- and y-coordinates of a position on the page.
Visibility Mode	Enumeration	Represents the visibility of a DOM element (hide or collapse).

The `Sys.UI` namespace has many useful classes so that you can manipulate DOM elements on your pages. Listing 4.5 uses the `DomElement` class to move a SPAN element to a new location on the page.

LISTING 4.5   Moving a SPAN Element to a New Location on the Page

```
<%@ Page Language="C#" %>

<!DOCTYPE html PUBLIC "-//W3C//DTD XHTML 1.0 Transitional//EN"
➥"http://www.w3.org/TR/xhtml1/DTD/xhtml1-transitional.dtd">

<script runat="server">

</script>

<html xmlns="http://www.w3.org/1999/xhtml">
<head runat="server">
    <title>Untitled Page</title>
    <script type="text/javascript">

      function pageLoad() {
      }

      //function to move the spn element to a new location
      function moveText(){
        Sys.UI.DomElement.setLocation(spn, 100, 250);
      }
    </script>
</head>
<body>
    <form id="form1" runat="server">
    <div>
        <asp:ScriptManager ID="ScriptManager1" runat="server" />
        <input type="button" id="btn" value="Click me to move the text below"
➥onclick="moveText();" />
        <br />
        <span id="spn">This is some text</span>
    </div>
    </form>
</body>
</html>
```

As you can see from Listing 4.5, there is a simple form with an HTML button and a SPAN element defined. When the button is clicked, a call is made to the moveText JavaScript method that will move the SPAN element:

```
function moveText(){
  Sys.UI.DomElement.setLocation(spn, 100, 250);
}
```

When you call the `Sys.UI.DomElement.setLocation` method, you are required to pass in the element that you want to move (in this instance, it is a SPAN called spn) and the x- and y-coordinates for the new location on the page.

Yes, you can accomplish the same thing by not using the `DomElement` class's `setLocation` method, but it requires you to write a few more lines of JavaScript. This allows you to move the element with only one line of code.

Sys.WebForms

The `Sys.WebForms` namespace provides classes that will help you with the partial page rendering functionality of ASP.NET AJAX. This namespace provides you with a lot of flexibility so that you can really make your ASP.NET AJAX pages "pop" and provide feedback to your users as elements on your page are posting back asynchronously. Table 4.8 describes the types that are defined by `Sys.WebForms`.

TABLE 4.8   Types Defined by the `Sys.WebForms` Namespace

Name	Description
BeginRequestEventArgs	Event arguments that get passed into the `BeginRequest` event of the `PageRequestManager`.
EndRequestEventArgs	Event arguments that get passed into the `EndRequest` event of the `PageRequestManager`.
InitializeRequestEventArgs	Event arguments that get passed into the `InitializeRequest` event of the `PageRequestManager`.
PageLoadedEventArgs	Event arguments that get passed into the `PageLoaded` event of the `PageRequestManager`.
PageLoadingEventArgs	Event arguments that get passed into the `PageLoading` event of the `PageRequestManager`.
PageRequestManager	The core class that is defined by the `Sys.WebForms` namespace. This class is used in conjunction with the ASP.NET AJAX UpdatePanel control and gives you the ability to code against the client-side events that happen with your ASP.NET AJAX-based requests back to the server.
Exceptions	Defines exceptions that can occur during the `BeginRequest`, `EndRequest`, `InitializeRequest`, `PageLoaded`, and `PageLoading` events of the `PageRequestManager`.

Listing 4.6 illustrates a page that uses the `PageRequestManager` class's `BeginRequest` and `EndRequest` events to display a message to the user to inform them that the page is loading something asynchronously when the button is clicked.

LISTING 4.6   Using the `PageRequestManager` Class's `BeginRequest` and `EndRequest` Events

```
<%@ Page Language="C#" %>


<!DOCTYPE html PUBLIC "-//W3C//DTD XHTML 1.0 Transitional//EN"
➥"http://www.w3.org/TR/xhtml1/DTD/xhtml1-transitional.dtd">


<script runat="server">

    protected void Button1_Click(object sender, EventArgs e)
    {
        System.Threading.Thread.Sleep(4000);
        Label1.Text = DateTime.Now.ToLongTimeString();
    }
</script>

<html xmlns="http://www.w3.org/1999/xhtml">
<head runat="server">
    <title>Untitled Page</title>
    <script type="text/javascript">

      function pageLoad() {
          Sys.WebForms.PageRequestManager.getInstance().add_
➥beginRequest(beginRequest);
          Sys.WebForms.PageRequestManager.getInstance().add_
➥endRequest(endRequest);
      }

      function beginRequest(sender, args){
        spnStatus.innerHTML = "Loading...";
      }

      function endRequest(sender, args){
        spnStatus.innerHTML = "Complete!";
      }

    </script>
</head>
<body>
    <form id="form1" runat="server">
    <div>
        <asp:ScriptManager ID="ScriptManager1" runat="server" />
    </div>
```

LISTING 4.6   Continued

```
    <asp:UpdatePanel ID="UpdatePanel1" runat="server">
        <ContentTemplate>
            <asp:Label ID="Label1" runat="server" Text="Label"></asp:Label>
            <br />
            <br />
            <asp:Button ID="Button1" runat="server"
➥onclick="Button1_Click" Text="Button" />
            <br />
            Status: <span id="spnStatus"></span>
        </ContentTemplate>
    </asp:UpdatePanel>
    </form>
</body>
</html>
```

The page that is defined in Listing 4.6 has an UpdatePanel that contains a button and a label. When the button is clicked, the server-side click event of the button sleeps for 4 seconds and then loads the current time into the label to simulate a long-running process.

If the users don't know that the page is updating asynchronously, they might click the button a number of times because they are not receiving any feedback that something is happening in the background. This can yield undesirable results especially if you are modifying items in a database (specifically on INSERT operations).

As a best practice, you should *always* let the end users know that something is happening asynchronously. This can be easily accomplished using the BeginRequest and EndRequest client-side events of the Sys.WebForms.PageRequestManager class. The following code excerpt highlights the way that you can hook into these events:

```
    function pageLoad() {
        Sys.WebForms.PageRequestManager.getInstance().add_
➥beginRequest(beginRequest);
        Sys.WebForms.PageRequestManager.getInstance().add_
➥endRequest(endRequest);
    }

    function beginRequest(sender, args){
      spnStatus.innerHTML = "Loading...";
    }

    function endRequest(sender, args){
      spnStatus.innerHTML = "Complete!";
    }
```

In the pageLoad event, you need to create event handlers for each event. In this example, the add_beginRequest and add_endRequest methods are called, and a handle to the appropriate JavaScript function that represents each event is passed into the method. When these events are raised (that is, the page is being updated asynchronously by the user clicking on the button in the UpdatePanel), the spnStatus control is updated to display a status to the user informing them that the page is being updated.

Using this simple addition to the UpdatePanel control provides you with a lot of flexibility and control when you use ASP.NET AJAX and will provide a lot of practical functionality to your page.

Summary

The ASP.NET AJAX Client API provides a lot of useful functionality that you should be familiar with. In this chapter, you learned about the capabilities that the ASP.NET AJAX Client API provides you as well as how you can utilize it in your applications to provide a lot of great functionality to your users and your applications.

CHAPTER 5

The UpdatePanel and Timer Controls

The UpdatePanel control is one of the more amazing controls of ASP.NET AJAX. It is a container control (similar to the ASP.NET Panel control) that enables you to use standard ASP.NET controls but will AJAX-enable them. In this chapter, you learn how to use the ASP.NET AJAX UpdatePanel control.

About the UpdatePanel Control

The UpdatePanel control enables you to quickly and easily create an AJAX-enabled application with little or no extra work. Like everything else in life, there are sacrifices you must make for the simplicity of using the UpdatePanel control. In the case of the UpdatePanel control, you sacrifice efficiency and bandwidth for ease of use.

Using this approach, there are tradeoffs depending on the type of application you are developing. You should consider other options, such as the features of the ScriptManager control and the client-side API, if you have a large number of users who need to use your page.

One of the major causes of performance problems with the UpdatePanel is the size of the data that gets sent to the server whenever an UpdatePanel is refreshing. When your page performs a postback via an UpdatePanel, it posts with the same data as a traditional ASP.NET web page; this includes the view state. If you recall from the previous chapters, one of the benefits of AJAX is the ability to reduce the amount of data that gets sent across the wire. If you plan to use UpdatePanels in your applications, you should first be aware of the overhead, and second, test, test, and test again. You should perform adequate performance tests with Visual Studio Team Test (or use another standard performance testing tool) before dropping your application into a production environment.

However, you shouldn't get discouraged with the UpdatePanel control because this advice is only for large enterprise applications. For applications with smaller user bases, the UpdatePanel control is perfect, and you can give your users an extremely rich user experience with not much work on your side.

In the next section, you learn how to use the UpdatePanel controls by looking at a few practical examples.

Using the UpdatePanel Control

As an ASP.NET developer, you will find the basics of using the UpdatePanel control very similar to the ASP.NET programming environment. Figure 5.1 illustrates the UpdatePanel control in the Visual Studio 2008 Control Toolbox.

FIGURE 5.1   UpdatePanel Control in the Toolbox.

Once you know where to locate the UpdatePanel on your page, you can drop it onto your ASP.NET web page and begin using AJAX. Listing 5.1 is a simple code example that uses an UpdatePanel control to suppress a postback when a call is made to populate a GridView

control with data from a database. Note that you will need to update the connection
string to reflect your database location, name, and credentials.

LISTING 5.1   UpdatePanel Basics

```
<%@ Page Language="C#" %>
<%@ Import Namespace="System.Data.SqlClient" %>
<%@ Import Namespace="System.Data" %>

<!DOCTYPE html PUBLIC "-//W3C//DTD XHTML 1.0 Transitional//EN"
 "http://www.w3.org/TR/xhtml1/DTD/xhtml1-transitional.dtd">

<script runat="server">

    protected void Page_Load(object sender, EventArgs e)
    {
        if (!this.Page.IsPostBack)
        {
        }
    }

    protected void btnGetData_Click(object sender, EventArgs e)
    {
        SqlConnection cn = new SqlConnection(
➥"Data Source=localhost;Initial Catalog=Northwind;User ID=sa;Password=password;");
        SqlCommand cmd = new SqlCommand("Customers_sel", cn);
        cmd.CommandType = System.Data.CommandType.StoredProcedure;
        SqlDataAdapter adp = new SqlDataAdapter(cmd);
        DataSet ds = new DataSet();
        try
        {
            adp.Fill(ds);
        }
        finally
        {
            adp.Dispose();
            cmd.Dispose();
            cn.Dispose();
        }
        this.gv.DataSource = ds.Tables[0].DefaultView;
        this.gv.DataBind();

    }
</script>

<html xmlns="http://www.w3.org/1999/xhtml">
```

LISTING 5.1   Continued

```
<head runat="server">
    <title>Untitled Page</title>
    <script type="text/javascript">

      function pageLoad() {
      }

    </script>
</head>
<body>
    <form id="form1" runat="server">
    <div>
        <asp:ScriptManager ID="ScriptManager1" runat="server" />
    </div>
    <asp:UpdatePanel ID="UpdatePanel1" runat="server">
        <ContentTemplate>
            <asp:Button ID="btnGetData" runat="server" onclick="btnGetData_Click"
                Text="Get Data" />
            <asp:GridView ID="gv" runat="server" BackColor="White"
                BorderColor="#999999" BorderStyle="None"
➥BorderWidth="1px" CellPadding="3"
                GridLines="Vertical">
                <footerstyle backcolor="#CCCCCC" forecolor="Black" />
                <rowstyle backcolor="#EEEEEE" forecolor="Black" />
                <pagerstyle backcolor="#999999"
➥forecolor="Black" horizontalalign="Center" />
                <selectedrowstyle backcolor="#008A8C" font-bold="True"
➥forecolor="White" />
                <headerstyle backcolor="#000084" font-bold="True"
➥forecolor="White" />
                <alternatingrowstyle backcolor="#DCDCDC" />
            </asp:GridView>
        </ContentTemplate>
    </asp:UpdatePanel>
    <asp:UpdateProgress runat="server" ID="prg"
➥AssociatedUpdatePanelID="UpdatePanel1" DisplayAfter="1">
        <ProgressTemplate>
            <img alt="" src="images/ajax-loader.gif"
➥style="width: 16px;height: 16px" />
        </ProgressTemplate>
    </asp:UpdateProgress>
    </form>
</body>
</html>
```

Figure 5.2 illustrates the rendered page after the grid has been populated by clicking the Get Data button.

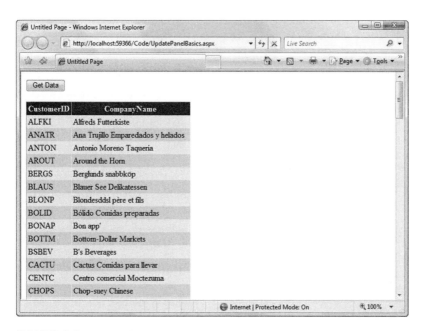

FIGURE 5.2   UpdatePanel Basics rendered page.

As you look through the code in Listing 5.1, notice that the only difference between the example and the way you would accomplish the same thing in traditional ASP.NET is that the server-side controls (the Button and GridView controls) are inside an UpdatePanel control. That's it! There are no JavaScript files that have to be maintained or proxies that have to be generated. That is the beauty of the UpdatePanel control.

Also notice that an UpdateProgress control is placed directly under the UpdatePanel control. One of the complaints often heard about the UpdatePanel control is that because there is no postback, users aren't always aware that their page has updated with the latest data. The UpdateProgress control can be associated with an UpdatePanel control and can provide the user with some visual feedback that the UpdatePanel is refreshing with data. In this example, an animated GIF file is displayed while the UpdatePanel is loading and then automatically gets hidden when the control is populated with data.

See how easy it is? If you have ever had to write or maintain AJAX code of *any* type and this is your first exposure to ASP.NET AJAX, then you are probably jumping with joy about the UpdatePanel's ease of use. In the next section, you learn about some of the advanced features of the UpdatePanel control that you can use in your applications.

Advanced Features of the UpdatePanel Control

Before you learn about the advanced features, it is important to learn what properties are exposed on the control itself. Table 5.1 describes each property of the UpdatePanel control.

TABLE 5.1   UpdatePanel Properties

Property	Description
ChildrenAsTriggers	Boolean that determines if controls contained inside the UpdatePanel will cause the UpdatePanel to refresh. Defalut value: True.
EnableViewState	Boolean that determines if the UpdatePanel will store ViewState. Default Value: True.
Triggers	Collection that stores events to external controls (outside of the UpdatePanel) that can cause the UpdatePanel to refresh itself.
UpdateMode	Determines how the UpdatePanel will refresh. Value can be either Always or Conditional. Default value: Always.
Visible	Boolean property of the UpdatePanel control that determines Visibility. Default value: True.
RenderMode	Determines how the control will render in the browser. Value can be Block, which will render a <div> tag, or Inline, which will render a <span> tag.
ID	Controls ID.

The properties are self-explanatory, but can save you a lot of time if you are using UpdatePanels in your application and you learn the capabilities and impacts of each property.

Triggers

In Listing 5.1, you learned how to create and use an UpdatePanel control. In the example, the UpdatePanel was essentially a self-contained unit that contained a Button and a GridView control. When the Button was clicked, the UpdatePanel refreshed itself when the Button's Click event was fired.

Often, especially when you are *really* using UpdatePanels, you might want the UpdatePanel (or multiple UpdatePanels) to refresh based on an event that occurred outside the UpdatePanel itself. This is especially important if you have multiple UpdatePanels on the page (which you learn about in the next section).

Triggers can be created easily for controls that are on the page, but not physically contained in the UpdatePanel control. You can create two types of triggers:

▶ AsyncPostBackTrigger—Refreshes the UpdatePanel asynchronously on postback.

► PostBackTrigger—Refreshes the UpdatePanel synchronously on postback. (For example, just do a regular postback, but refresh the UpdatePanel.)

NOTE

Because this is an AJAX book, only `AsynchPostBackTrigger` will be covered in the next example.

You can configure triggers inline with code or by clicking the ellipsis on the Triggers collection property in the Properties window in Visual Studio. If you click the ellipsis, you will see a dialog box, as shown in Figure 5.3.

FIGURE 5.3   Adding a trigger to an UpdatePanel.

As you can see in Figure 5.3, a trigger is set to refresh the UpdatePanel control when the Click event is fired from a Button control named `btnUpdate`. It is important to note that even though this particular example has only one trigger, you can have many triggers configured to refresh the UpdatePanel; you likely will have many controls on your page that can cause the UpdatePanel to be refreshed.

Listing 5.2 is an example of using a trigger to refresh an UpdatePanel control.

LISTING 5.2   Using Triggers

```
<%@ Page Language="C#" %>
<%@ Import Namespace="System.Data.SqlClient" %>
<%@ Import Namespace="System.Data" %>

<!DOCTYPE html PUBLIC "-//W3C//DTD XHTML 1.0 Transitional//EN"
"http://www.w3.org/TR/xhtml1/DTD/xhtml1-transitional.dtd">
```

LISTING 5.2   Continued

```
<script runat="server">

    protected void btnUpdate_Click(object sender, EventArgs e)
    {
        SqlConnection cn = new SqlConnection(
"Data Source=localhost;Initial Catalog=Northwind;User ID=sa;Password=password;");
        SqlCommand cmd = new SqlCommand("Customers_sel", cn);
        cmd.CommandType = System.Data.CommandType.StoredProcedure;
        SqlDataAdapter adp = new SqlDataAdapter(cmd);
        DataSet ds = new DataSet();
        try
        {
            adp.Fill(ds);
        }
        finally
        {
            adp.Dispose();
            cmd.Dispose();
            cn.Dispose();
        }
        this.gv.DataSource = ds.Tables[0].DefaultView;
        this.gv.DataBind();

    }
</script>

<html xmlns="http://www.w3.org/1999/xhtml">
<head runat="server">
    <title>Untitled Page</title>
    <script type="text/javascript">

      function pageLoad() {
      }

    </script>
</head>
<body>
    <form id="form1" runat="server">
    <div>
        <asp:ScriptManager ID="ScriptManager1" runat="server" />
    </div>
    <asp:Button runat="server" ID="btnUpdate" Text="Update"
        onclick="btnUpdate_Click" />
    <br />
    <br />
```

```
    <asp:UpdatePanel ID="up" runat="server">
        <Triggers>
            <asp:AsyncPostBackTrigger ControlID="btnUpdate" EventName="Click" />
        </Triggers>
        <ContentTemplate>
            <asp:Label ID="lbl" runat="server"></asp:Label>
            <asp:GridView ID="gv" runat="server" BackColor="White"
➥BorderColor="#999999"
➥BorderStyle="None" BorderWidth="1px" CellPadding="3" GridLines="Vertical">
                <footerstyle backcolor="#CCCCCC" forecolor="Black" />
                <rowstyle backcolor="#EEEEEE" forecolor="Black" />
                <pagerstyle backcolor="#999999"
➥forecolor="Black" horizontalalign="Center" />
                <selectedrowstyle backcolor="#008A8C"
➥font-bold="True" forecolor="White" />
                <headerstyle backcolor="#000084" font-bold="True"
➥forecolor="White" />
                <alternatingrowstyle backcolor="#DCDCDC" />
            </asp:GridView>
        </ContentTemplate>
    </asp:UpdatePanel>
    </form>
</body>
</html>
```

In Listing 5.2, an `AsyncPostBackTrigger` has been defined on the UpdatePanel control and will be fired by the Click event of the `btnUpdate` Button control. This allows the UpdatePanel control to refresh asynchronously when the Button is clicked.

Again, this is a very useful technique to use when you want to refresh multiple UpdatePanel controls on your page when the user performs a task (such as clicking a "refresh" button). This can be accomplished by simply adding triggers to the triggers collection of the UpdatePanel control that will get fired when you want the UpdatePanel controls to refresh.

Multiple UpdatePanel Controls on a Single Page

Often, you will have multiple UpdatePanel controls on your pages at the same time. A common practice is to host each UpdatePanel in separate ASP.NET user controls (.ASCX files). This enables you to have multiple units on your page that can refresh either individually or together as a unit (using triggers). In Listing 5.3, you learn how to create master-detail ASP.NET user controls in which the master control communicates with the details control to refresh its data with detail records based on a user selection. Figure 5.4 illustrates a sequence diagram of the flow that will occur between the two user controls (named ucCustomers.ascx and ucCustomerOrders.ascx).

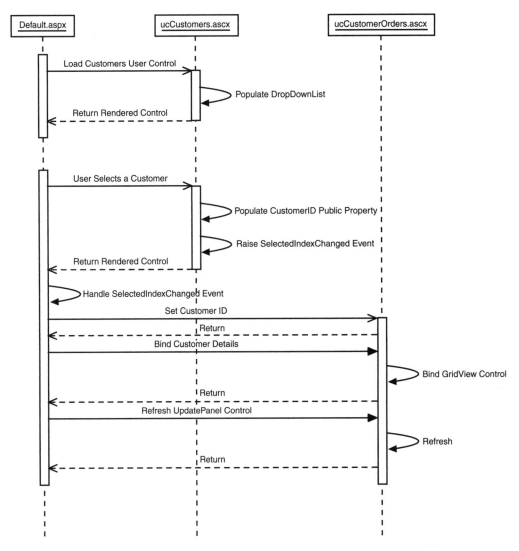

FIGURE 5.4   User control sequence diagram.

Figure 5.5 illustrates the page that will get rendered in the example in Listing 5.3. This helps you to visualize what the code will actually be doing as you read ahead into the next example.

Looking first at the ucCustomers.ascx file, you will notice that a few of the UpdatePanel's properties and methods have been exposed publicly through the control: UpdatePanelUpdateMode and Update.

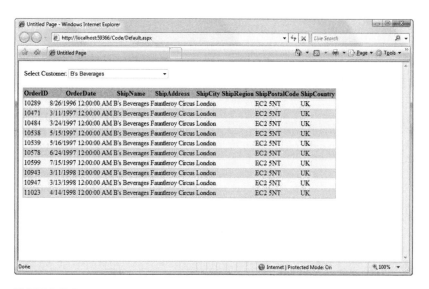

FIGURE 5.5   Master/Detail UpdatePanel controls.

UpdatePanelUpdateMode allows you to dynamically control how your UpdatePanel updates. This can be set to the values of Always and Conditional. This value is set to Always in the ucCustomers.ascx user control because you will want the user control to update automatically every time the user selects a customer from the DropDownList control.

LISTING 5.3   ucCustomers.ascx

```
<%@ Control Language="C#" ClassName="ucCustomers" %>
<%@ Import Namespace="System.Data.SqlClient" %>
<%@ Import Namespace="System.Data" %>
<%@ Import Namespace="System.Web" %>
<%@ Import Namespace="System.Web.UI" %>
<%@ Import Namespace="System.Web.UI.WebControls" %>
<script runat="server">

    public UpdatePanelUpdateMode UpdateMode
    {
        get { return this.upCustomers.UpdateMode; }
        set { this.upCustomers.UpdateMode = value; }
    }

    public void Update()
    {
        this.upCustomers.Update();
    }
```

LISTING 5.3   Continued

```
    public string CustomerID
    {
        get { return this.ddlCustomers.SelectedValue; }
    }

    protected void Page_Load(object sender, EventArgs e)
    {
        if (!this.Page.IsPostBack)
        {
            SqlConnection cn = new SqlConnection(
➥"Data Source=localhost;Initial Catalog=Northwind;User ID=sa;Password=password;");
            SqlCommand cmd = new SqlCommand("Customers_sel", cn);
            cmd.CommandType = System.Data.CommandType.StoredProcedure;
            SqlDataAdapter adp = new SqlDataAdapter(cmd);
            DataSet ds = new DataSet();
            try
            {
                adp.Fill(ds);
                this.ddlCustomers.DataSource = ds.Tables[0].DefaultView;
                this.ddlCustomers.DataValueField = "CustomerID";
                this.ddlCustomers.DataTextField = "CompanyName";
            }
            finally
            {
                adp.Dispose();
                cmd.Dispose();
                cn.Dispose();
            }
            this.ddlCustomers.DataBind();
            this.ddlCustomers.Items.Insert(0, "Select a customer");
        }
    }
    public event EventHandler SelectedIndexChanged;

    protected void indexChanged(object sender, EventArgs e)
    {
        if (SelectedIndexChanged != null)
        {
            SelectedIndexChanged(this, e);
        }
    }
}
</script>

<asp:UpdatePanel ID="upCustomers" runat="server">
    <ContentTemplate>
```

```
        <table>
            <tr>
                <td>Select Customer:</td>
                <td><asp:DropDownList runat="server" ID="ddlCustomers"
 AutoPostBack="true" OnSelectedIndexChanged="indexChanged" >
</asp:DropDownList></td>
            </tr>
        </table>
    </ContentTemplate>
</asp:UpdatePanel>
```

The key to the control in Listing 5.3 is that you need to create a custom event that will get fired when the user selects a customer. This can be done by creating an event handler for the `OnSelectedIndexChanged` event of the DropDownList control and firing the custom event when the user selects a customer from the DropDownList. The custom event, `SelectedIndexChanged`, is handled by the ucCustomerOrders.ascx control, which tells the details control when to display the selected customer's orders records.

The final property that has been defined, `CustomerID`, is used to expose which customer is selected in the DropDownList. This will be used in the ucCustomerOrders.ascx file to determine which customer's details to display.

Listing 5.4 illustrates the ucCustomerOrders.ascx user control.

LISTING 5.4   ucCustomerOrders.ascx

```
<%@ Control Language="C#" ClassName="ucCustomerOrders" %>
<%@ Import Namespace="System.Data" %>
<%@ Import Namespace="System.Data.SqlClient" %>
<script runat="server">
    private string _customerID = string.Empty;

    public UpdatePanelUpdateMode UpdateMode
    {
        get { return this.upCustomerOrders.UpdateMode; }
        set { this.upCustomerOrders.UpdateMode = value; }
    }

    public void Update()
    {
        this.upCustomerOrders.Update();
    }

    public string CustomerID
    {
        get { return this._customerID; }
```

LISTING 5.4   Continued

```
        set { this._customerID = value; }
    }

    protected void Page_Load(object sender, EventArgs e)
    {
        if (!this.Page.IsPostBack)
        {
        }
    }

    public void BindGrid()
    {
        SqlConnection cn = new SqlConnection(
➥"Data Source=localhost;Initial Catalog=Northwind;User ID=sa;Password=password;");
        SqlCommand cmd = new SqlCommand("CustomerOrders_sel", cn);
        cmd.CommandType = System.Data.CommandType.StoredProcedure;
        cmd.Parameters.Add(new SqlParameter("@CustomerID", this._customerID));
        SqlDataAdapter adp = new SqlDataAdapter(cmd);
        DataSet ds = new DataSet();
        try
        {
            adp.Fill(ds);
            this.gvOrders.DataSource = ds.Tables[0].DefaultView;
        }
        finally
        {
            adp.Dispose();
            cmd.Dispose();
            cn.Dispose();
        }
        this.gvOrders.DataBind();

    }
</script>
<asp:UpdatePanel ID="upCustomerOrders" runat="server">
    <ContentTemplate>
        <asp:GridView ID="gvOrders" runat="server" BackColor="LightGoldenrodYellow"
            BorderColor="Tan" BorderWidth="1px" CellPadding="2" ForeColor="Black"
            GridLines="None">
            <footerstyle backcolor="Tan" />
            <pagerstyle backcolor="PaleGoldenrod" forecolor="DarkSlateBlue"
                horizontalalign="Center" />
            <selectedrowstyle backcolor="DarkSlateBlue" forecolor="GhostWhite" />
            <headerstyle backcolor="Tan" font-bold="True" />
            <alternatingrowstyle backcolor="PaleGoldenrod" />
```

```
        </asp:GridView>
      </ContentTemplate>
</asp:UpdatePanel>
```

In the ucCustomerOrders.ascx file, several properties and methods have been defined. As with the ucCustomers.ascx user control, the UpdatePanelUpdateMode property and Update method are publicly exposed in the user control from the UpdatePanel control. The only difference is that the UpdateMode of the UpdatePanel control will need to be set to Conditional. This is because you want to refresh the UpdatePanel dynamically when a user selects a customer's record from the DropDownList defined in Listing 5.3. This is only possible if the UpdateMode is set to Conditional; otherwise, the control will update when the page asynchronously posts back instead of allowing you to control when that actually occurs.

A CustomerID property also has been defined in the control. This will be set by the Default.aspx file when the SelectedIndexChanged event is fired (in other words, when the user selects a customer record from the DropDownList control). This property is used to pass in which customer's orders to display in the GridView control and is used as a parameter in the stored procedure that is called in the BindGrid method.

After you have written your user controls (as defined in Listings 5.3 and 5.4), you are ready to display them on an ASPX page. In Listing 5.5, Default.aspx is used to host your user controls.

LISTING 5.5   Default.aspx

```
<%@ Page Language="C#" %>

<%@ Register src="ucCustomers.ascx" tagname="ucCustomers" tagprefix="uc1" %>

<%@ Register src="ucCustomerOrders.ascx" tagname="ucCustomerOrders"
tagprefix="uc2" %>

<!DOCTYPE html PUBLIC "-//W3C//DTD XHTML 1.0 Transitional//EN"
"http://www.w3.org/TR/xhtml1/DTD/xhtml1-transitional.dtd">

<script runat="server">

    protected void Page_Load(object sender, EventArgs e)
    {
        if (!this.Page.IsPostBack)
        {
            this.UpdateCustomerOrders();
        }
    }
    protected void indexChanged(object sender, EventArgs e)
```

LISTING 5.5   Continued

```
    {
        this.UpdateCustomerOrders();
    }

    private void UpdateCustomerOrders()
    {
        ucCustomerOrders1.CustomerID = ucCustomers1.CustomerID;
        ucCustomerOrders1.BindGrid();
        ucCustomerOrders1.Update();

    }
</script>

<html xmlns="http://www.w3.org/1999/xhtml">
<head runat="server">
    <title>Untitled Page</title>
    <script type="text/javascript">

      function pageLoad() {
      }

    </script>
</head>
<body>
    <form id="form1" runat="server">
    <div>
        <asp:ScriptManager ID="ScriptManager1" runat="server" />

    </div>

    <uc1:ucCustomers ID="ucCustomers1" runat="server"
➥OnSelectedIndexChanged="indexChanged" UpdateMode="Conditional" />
<br />
    <uc2:ucCustomerOrders ID="ucCustomerOrders1"
runat="server" UpdateMode="Conditional" />
    </form>
</body>
</html>
```

There are three factors that are core to Default.aspx. First, it is used to display the controls. You can see that the controls are simply laid out in the body section of the form. Second, an event handler is created for the IndexChanged event of the ucCustomers control. This is the custom event that is defined by that control itself, which is raised when the user selects a customer record. When this event is fired, a call is made to the third important factor of the page, the `UpdateCustomerOrders` method.

First, the `UpdateCustomerOrders` method sets the `CustomerID` property of the ucCustomerOrders.ascx control to the value of the selected customer of the ucCustomers.ascx file. Then it calls the `BindGrid` method, which will bind the GridView control to the selected customer's order records. Finally, a call is made to the `Update` method, which causes the UpdatePanel control to refresh asynchronously and display the selected customer's orders.

The principle take-away from this section should be that there isn't much difference in using multiple UpdatePanel controls on the page than not using UpdatePanels at all. As long as you remember that you need to Update (or refresh) the UpdatePanel control, you will hopefully get the results and user experience that you expect the first time, every time.

The Timer Control

The Timer control is a very useful control because it enables you to create a postback at a defined interval. It is similar in nature to the Timer control used in Windows Forms.

The Timer control contains four properties and one event, as shown in Table 5.2.

TABLE 5.2   Timer Control Properties and Events

Property	Description
Enabled	Enables/Disables the Timer. If disabled, the Timer's `OnTick` event will not fire.
EnabledViewState	Enables/Disables ViewState for the Timer control.
Interval	Number of time in milliseconds that the `OnTick` event will fire.
ID	ID of the Timer control.
Event	**Description**
OnTick	The `OnTick` event is fired after the amount of time in the `Interval` property has lapsed.

You can use the Timer control together with an UpdatePanel control by using the following two approaches. First, the UpdatePanel can contain a Timer control and the asynchronous updates will be encapsulated in the UpdatePanel itself. This is the approach that you want to use if you would like your UpdatePanel to update as a self-contained unit.

The second approach (and the one you'll see in the example in the next section) involves defining your Timer control outside the context of the UpdatePanel and refreshing the UpdatePanel with a trigger. This scenario is more common because it will allow you to update multiple UpdatePanels on the page, having only one Timer control defined.

In the next section, you learn how to use the Timer control by refreshing an UpdatePanel control with a trigger.

Using the Timer Control with Partial-Page Rendering

The easiest way to look at the Timer control is to concentrate on the control itself rather than complex code that is used to update something on the page. With this in mind, the example in Listing 5.6 uses a timer to add random numbers to a ListBox control that is defined inside an UpdatePanel control using a trigger on the UpdatePanel.

Figure 5.6 illustrates an example of what the page will look like when it is rendered.

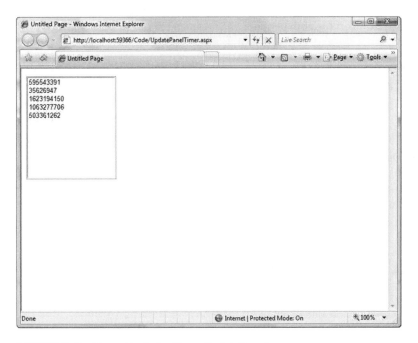

FIGURE 5.6   Timer Control with an UpdatePanel.

Using the Timer is as simple as the page shown in Figure 5.6. Listing 5.6 is the code used to render the page shown in Figure 5.6.

LISTING 5.6   Using the Timer Control

```
<%@ Page Language="C#" %>


<!DOCTYPE html PUBLIC "-//W3C//DTD XHTML 1.0 Transitional//EN"
"http://www.w3.org/TR/xhtml1/DTD/xhtml1-transitional.dtd">
<html>
<script runat="server">
```

```
    protected void tmr_Tick(object sender, EventArgs e)
    {
        Random r = new Random();
        lbRandomNumbers.Items.Add(r.Next().ToString());
    }
</script>
<head>
<title>Untitled Page</title>
    <script type="text/javascript">

    function pageLoad() {
    }

    </script>
</head>
<body>
    <form id="form1" runat="server">
    <div>
        <asp:ScriptManager ID="ScriptManager1" runat="server" />
        <asp:Timer ID="tmr" runat="server" Interval="1000" ontick="tmr_Tick">
        </asp:Timer>
        <asp:UpdatePanel ID="uPanel" runat="server">
            <ContentTemplate>
                <asp:ListBox runat="server" ID="lbRandomNumbers" Height="202px"
Width="179px"></asp:ListBox>
            </ContentTemplate>
            <Triggers>
                <asp:AsyncPostBackTrigger ControlID="tmr" EventName="Tick" />
            </Triggers>
        </asp:UpdatePanel>
    </div>
    </form>
</body>
</html>
```

The things you should focus on in this code example are the Timer control, the Tick event, and the Trigger that is defined on the UpdatePanel control.

The Timer control is set to update every 1,000 milliseconds, or every second. You should be *very* careful when setting the Timer's Interval property because you do not want the timer to fire its Tick event before the previous call to the Tick event has finished. So, rule number one of the Timer control is to keep the logic in your Tick events simple and efficient. Because the code example is simply adding a random number to a ListBox on the page, 1,000 milliseconds should be plenty of time for this process to finish before another Tick event is fired.

Finally, a trigger is configured on the UpdatePanel control to fire when the timer's `Tick` event is fired. This enables the UpdatePanel to refresh asynchronously when the `Tick` event is fired.

The Timer control is very useful and provides a lot of functionality to you as a web developer.

Summary

In this chapter, you learned how to use the UpdatePanel and Timer controls in your ASP.NET applications. Each control has its use in the ASP.NET AJAX world and can save you a lot of time and effort to get specific functionality embedded into the user experience of your ASP.NET web pages.

CHAPTER 6

Advanced Techniques with the ASP.NET AJAX PageRequestManager Object

Using the PageRequestManager Object

The PageRequestManager object is an object that you should be extremely familiar with if you are doing anything with ASP.NET AJAX. At the core, the concepts of AJAX are simply a set of asynchronous requests that are happening on your page.

When you are using some of the server-side controls that ship with ASP.NET 3.5 AJAX such as the UpdatePanel, you are often abstracted from each HTTP request that is getting generated by the UpdatePanel. This is both good and bad. The "good" is that you can just drop an UpdatePanel control on your page and don't have to write much code (if *any*) to make your page post back asynchronously. The "bad" is that without writing code, you are stuck with the out-of-box functionality that is provided by the UpdatePanel. This means that you do not have the flexibility to trap for specific events or even cancel an asynchronous postback, if needed.

The client-side ASP.NET AJAX object model contains an object called the PageRequestManager that can help you manage these requests that are being generated by the server-side ASP.NET AJAX controls. This object encapsulates a lot of very powerful functionality that you can use to ensure that your requests are being sent as expected.

Table 6.1 describes the PageRequestManager's properties, methods, and events.

The `PageRequestManager` object is a singleton object, so you can't just create an instance of it and start using it. You need to call the `getInstance` static method of the `PageRequestManager` object itself to create an instance of the object, as demonstrated in the following code sample:

```
var prm = Sys.WebForms.PageRequestManager.getInstance();
```

By getting the current instance of the `PageRequestManager` object, you can then start to use the methods and properties that are defined by the object itself.

TABLE 6.1   Properties, Methods, and Events of `PageRequestManager`

Name	Type	Description
beginRequest	Event	Event that gets fired when an HTTP request begins
endRequest	Event	Event that gets fired when an HTTP request ends (or completes)
initializeRequest	Event	Event that gets fired when an HTTP request is initialized
pageLoaded	Event	Event that gets fired when the page has been loaded after a `PostBack`
pageLoading	Event	Event that gets fired when the page is loading after a `PostBack`
add_beginRequest	Method	Method that adds an event handler for the beginRequest event
add_endRequest	Method	Method that adds an event handler for the endRequest event
add_InitializeRequest	Method	Method that adds an event handler for the InitializeRequest event
add_pageLoaded	Method	Method that adds an event handler for the pageLoaded event
add_pageLoading	Method	Method that adds an event handler for the pageLoading event
abortPostBack	Method	Method that aborts the asynchronous `PostBack`
dispose	Method	Method that disposes the object
getInstance	Method	Method that gets the current running instance of the `PageRequestManager` object
isInAsyncPostBack	Property	Boolean property that gets whether the page is currently in an asynchronous `PostBack`

A Practical Example of the PageRequestManager Object

When you use the PageRequestManager object, you will likely use every available property, method, and event because they provide a lot of value to the objects that are executing on your page. You can see this accomplished in Listing 6.1.

LISTING 6.1   Default.aspx

```
<%@ Page Language="C#" %>


<!DOCTYPE html PUBLIC "-//W3C//DTD XHTML 1.0 Transitional//EN"
 "http://www.w3.org/TR/xhtml1/DTD/xhtml1-transitional.dtd">


<script runat="server">

    protected void Button1_Click(object sender, EventArgs e)
    {
        System.Threading.Thread.Sleep(4000);
        Label1.Text = (int.Parse(TextBox1.Text) +
int.Parse(TextBox2.Text)).ToString();
    }
</script>


<html xmlns="http://www.w3.org/1999/xhtml">
<head runat="server">
    <title>Untitled Page</title>
    <script type="text/javascript">

      function pageLoad() {
        var prm = Sys.WebForms.PageRequestManager.getInstance();

        //add handlers for client-side ASP.NET AJAX Events
        prm.add_beginRequest(beginRequest);
        prm.add_endRequest(endRequest);
        prm.add_initializeRequest(initializeRequest);
        prm.add_pageLoaded(pageLoaded);
        prm.add_pageLoading(pageLoading);
      }

      //begin request event handler
      function beginRequest(sender, args){
        spnStatus.innerHTML = 'Begin request';
      }
```

LISTING 6.1   Continued

```
      //end request event handler
      function endRequest(sender, args){
        spnStatus.innerHTML = 'Complete!';
      }

      //initialize request event handler
      function initializeRequest(sender, args){
          var prm = Sys.WebForms.PageRequestManager.getInstance();
          if (prm.get_isInAsyncPostBack() & args.get_postBackElement().id ==
➥'btnCancel') {
              prm.abortPostBack();
          }
          else if (prm.get_isInAsyncPostBack() &
args.get_postBackElement().id == 'btnSubmit') {
              args.set_cancel(true);
              spnStatus.innerHTML = 'Still processing, please wait...';
          }
          else if (!prm.get_isInAsyncPostBack() &
args.get_postBackElement().id == 'btnSubmit') {
              spnStatus.innerHTML = 'Getting Results';
          }

      }

      //page loaded event handler
      function pageLoaded(sender, args){
        spnStatus.innerHTML = 'Page Loaded';
      }

      //page loading event handler
      function pageLoading(sender, args){
        spnStatus.innerHTML = 'Page Loading';
      }
    </script>
</head>
<body>
    <form id="form1" runat="server">
    <div>
        <asp:ScriptManager ID="ScriptManager1" runat="server" />
        <asp:UpdatePanel ID="UpdatePanel1" runat="server">
            <ContentTemplate>
                <table>
                    <tr>
                        <td>Number 1:</td>
                        <td>
```

```
                            <asp:TextBox ID="TextBox1" runat="server">
➡</asp:TextBox>
</td>
                        </tr>
                        <tr>
                            <td>Number 2:</td>
                            <td>
                                <asp:TextBox ID="TextBox2" runat="server">
➡</asp:TextBox>
</td>
                        </tr>
                        <tr>
                            <td>Result:</td>
                            <td>
                                <asp:Label ID="Label1" runat="server"></asp:Label></td>
                        </tr>
                        <tr>
                            <td><asp:Button ID="btnCancel" runat="server"
Text="Cancel" /></td>
                            <td>
                                <asp:Button ID="btnSubmit" runat="server"
Text="Get Result" onclick="Button1_Click" /></td>
                        </tr>
                        <tr>
                            <td colspan="2"><span id="spnStatus"></span></td>
                        </tr>
                    </table>
                </ContentTemplate>
            </asp:UpdatePanel>
        </div>
        </form>
</body>
</html>
```

The functionality of the page is quite simple. There are two TextBoxes that allow you to type in two numbers, which get added together and the result is returned in a Label control. To simulate a long-running process, when the user clicks the Get Result button to add the numbers, a 4000 millisecond delay has been implemented by forcing the main thread to sleep in the Get Result button's click event. By design, this is a very simple page so that you can focus on the inner workings of the PageRequestManager object.

Allowing your users to execute asynchronous requests with ASP.NET AJAX could introduce a few issues in your applications that you do not have to handle with traditional, synchronous web applications. For example, in a synchronous web page, when the user clicks a command button, the page posts back and the user is forced to wait until the page is reloaded in the browser before they can complete another action. In an asynchronous web page, when the user clicks a command button, it executes the code behind the button and if the user immediately clicks it again, it starts another asynchronous request. If the user clicks the button a third time, a third request is fired. In the example illustrated by Listing 6.1, this type of behavior doesn't present a problem, but it could become problematic when you are executing code that updates a database. You can easily prevent the user from making multiple requests as well as give them a status that their first request is still processing.

You first need to configure event handlers for each of the PageRequestManager's events that get fired. In this example, this is done in the pageLoad JavaScript event. Each of the add_*eventHandler* methods are invoked to set up the event handlers of the PageRequestManager object.

If you notice the signature of each of the event-handler methods, you can see that they all have sender and args arguments, similar to a server-side event where sender represents the object that caused the asynchronous PostBack and where args represents any arguments that are available for each asynchronous PostBack.

The beginRequest, endRequest, pageLoading, and pageLoaded events simply update the status label (named spnStatus) to inform the user of the request status. The work to prevent a user from firing off multiple requests is contained within the initializeRequest event, which gets fired when the request is initialized and before the request is sent to the server.

In the initalizeRequest method, you need to check for four things:

▶ Is an asynchronous PostBack being processed? This is checked every time.

▶ Is the user canceling the request?

▶ Is the user trying to reexecute the request?

▶ Is the user executing the request for the first time?

The following code excerpt from the initializeRequest event illustrates these four checks:

```
        var prm = Sys.WebForms.PageRequestManager.getInstance();
        if (prm.get_isInAsyncPostBack() & args.get_postBackElement().id ==
➥'btnCancel') {
            prm.abortPostBack();
        }
        else if (prm.get_isInAsyncPostBack() &
args.get_postBackElement().id == 'btnSubmit') {
            args.set_cancel(true);
            spnStatus.innerHTML = 'Still processing, please wait...';
        }
        else if (!prm.get_isInAsyncPostBack() &
args.get_postBackElement().id == 'btnSubmit') {
            spnStatus.innerHTML = 'Getting Results';
        }
```

You need to check to see if the page is executing an asynchronous `PostBack`, so you can see this check in each block of the `IF` statement. If the user is canceling the request, you can call the `abortPostBack` method of the `PageRequestManager` object to cancel the request that is being executed. Note that if you are updating a database, this does not roll back the transaction that is being fired off and you will need to handle this in the server-side method.

If the user is trying to reexecute their request, you need to cancel the request that is getting initialized. You can determine this by first checking to see if an asynchronous `PostBack` is in process and then checking to see if the button that was clicked was the Get Results button. If both of these conditions are true, the user has clicked the button again and is trying to reexecute the request. In this instance, you need to cancel the request to prevent another request of the same type from being fired. This is done by making a call to the `args.set_cancel` method and then informing the user that their request is still being processed. Figure 6.1 illustrates the results of a user trying to reexecute a request.

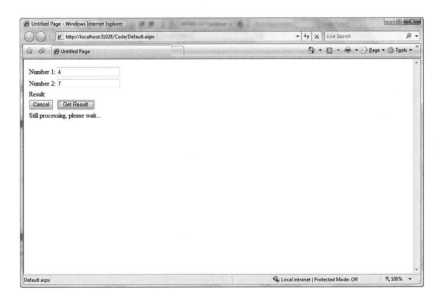

FIGURE 6.1   Preventing a user from reexecuting a request.

Finally, if this is the first request that is being sent (notice in the last `IF` statement that a check is made to ensure that an asynchronous `PostBack` is not executing by calling the `!prm.get_isInAsyncPostBack` property), you should update the current status to inform the user that their request is being processed.

The `initializeRequest` event handler is the core of this example because it allows you to check the status of a request that is either in progress, cancel a request, or allow a request to be fired for the first time in a process. In this section, you have learned how to efficiently use the `PageRequestManager` object to provide rich functionality to your ASP.NET AJAX applications.

Figure 6.2 illustrates the page as it is displayed when the request has finished executing.

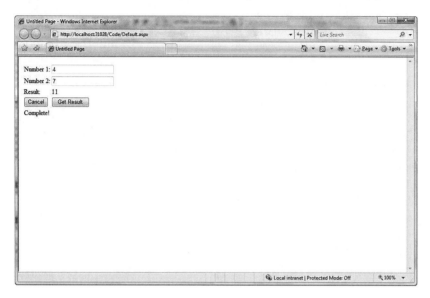

FIGURE 6.2   All requests have completed executing.

Summary

The `PageRequestManager` object is fundamental to doing any advanced (or production-ready) ASP.NET AJAX development. In this chapter, you have learned about using the ASP.NET AJAX `PageRequestManager` object and its properties, methods, and events. This chapter also presented a very real-world example of suppressing a user's action to execute multiple asynchronous requests when they click a command button while an asynchronous request is being processed.

CHAPTER 7

Using the ASP.NET AJAX Control Toolkit

This chapter is going to be a fun ride as you learn how to make a big impact with your user community with not a lot of effort. Up until now, you have been learning about AJAX and the features available to you as an ASP.NET developer from an AJAX perspective. Although this foundation is essential in understanding the fundamentals of what is happening behind the scenes, it has touched only moderately on the user experience.

The ASP.NET AJAX Control Toolkit is an open source project that is hosted on CodePlex (http://www.codeplex.com/Wiki/View.aspx?ProjectName=AtlasControlToolkit). Although Microsoft obviously has contributed much to the effort, the ASP.NET AJAX Control Toolkit is a community effort to provide a suite of controls that extend the existing functionality of ASP.NET and ASP.NET AJAX. At the time that this chapter is being written, there are 37 controls in the ASP.NET AJAX Control Toolkit that likely will change in the future as more controls and functionality are added to the suite of controls.

The ASP.NET AJAX Control Toolkit focuses mostly on the user experience (UX) aspects of ASP.NET AJAX. Most (if not all) of the controls help you to easily provide a richer user experience for your users by encapsulating much of the functionality in a nice assembly that you can use with either Visual Studio (2005 and 2008) or Visual Web Developer.

NOTE

All examples in this chapter are created with Visual Studio 2008 but work just as easily in Visual Studio 2005 and Visual Web Developer.

ASP.NET AJAX Control Toolkit: The Controls

So what does the ASP.NET AJAX Control Toolkit contain? Two categories of controls are available: the full blown AJAX-based controls and AJAX extenders, which enable you to AJAX-ify the standard ASP.NET controls. Table 7.1 lists and briefly describes the controls, which will be useful when you are learning their capabilities.

As you begin to use the ASP.NET AJAX Control Toolkit, you will often use many of these controls on your page so that you can provide the consumers of your site with a more robust user experience. For example, you might want to use an Accordion control to display multiple collapsible panels on your page. In each "header," you could use a ToggleButtonExtender control to display an up arrow when a section in the Accordion is expanded and a down arrow when a section is collapsed. At the same time, you could also display messages to your user with the PopupControlExtender control.

TABLE 7.1   ASP.NET AJAX Control Toolkit Controls

Control	Description
Accordion	Enables you to define an accordion style of content in which your users select from a list of headers, and the content of that header item is displayed as the other headers' content is hidden by an animation.
AccordionPane	Defines a pane for content displayed by the Accordion control.
AlwaysVisibleControlExtender	Extends the Panel control. Displays a panel that is always visible on the page, even when you scroll the browser.
AnimationExtender	Allows you to define XML-based animations for your controls.
CalendarExtender	Extends the TextBox control. Displays a Calendar control when a defined TextBox has focus.
CascadingDropDown	Provides the functionality of having related updates when values are selected from DropDowns.
CollapsiblePanelExtender	Extends the Panel control. Enables you to dynamically expand/collapse a panel area on your page.
ConfirmButtonExtender	Extends the Button control. Enables you to specify an "Are you sure?" type confirmation message to your users when they click a button.
DragPanelExtender	Extends the Panel control. Enables you to easily drag and drop panels on your page.
DropDownExtender	Extends the TextBox control. Provides the functionality of a "panel" that is dropped down from the textbox in which you can select values for the textbox.

TABLE 7.1   Continued

Control	Description
DropShadowExtender	Extends the Panel control. Provides a drop shadow for your panel controls.
DynamicPopulateExtender	Extends a web control by calling a web service and populating the control with the results of the web service.
FilteredTextBoxExtender	Extends the TextBox control. Enables you to filter the entry of values that a user can type into a textbox.
HoverMenuExtender	Extends the Panel control. Provides the functionality to display a custom menu when you hover over an item on the page.
ListSearchExtender	Extends the ListBox control. Enables users to search the contents of a ListBox by typing the values they are looking for (traditionally, the ListBox searches based *only* on the first character that is typed).
MaskedEditExtender	Extends the TextBox control. Provides the functionality similar to a Windows Forms MaskedEdit TextBox.
MaskedEditValidator	Represents a validator control that can be attached to the MaskedEditExtender control.
ModalPopupExtender	Extends a Panel control. Enables you to display an invisible panel as a modal popup.
MutuallyExclusiveCheckBoxExtender	Extends the CheckBox control. Provides the functionality to make CheckBoxes mutually exclusive (like radio buttons).
NoBot	Provides functionality to block web bots that try to use your page to submit entries to your site.
NumericUpDownExtender	Extends the TextBox control. Enables you to associate increment/decrement buttons for setting numeric values of TextBoxes.
PagingBulletedListExtender	Extends the Panel control. Provides the functionality of a bulleted list that pages.
PasswordStrength	Extends the TextBox control. Enables you to check password strength when users are setting a password field and provide users with feedback on their password strength.
PopupControlExtender	Extends the TextBox control. Provides the functionality of showing a hidden Panel control as a dropdown for selecting values for a TextBox.

TABLE 7.1   Continued

Control	Description
Rating	Represents an AJAX rating control, similar to what you see on popular sites such as Amazon.com.
ReorderList	Extends the Panel control. Enables you to drag and drop items in a list to change the order.
ResizableControlExtender	Can extend many different controls. Provides the functionality of allowing the user to resize a control on the page.
RoundedCornersExtender	Extends the Panel control. Allows you to provide rounded corners for your Panel controls on your page.
SliderExtender	Extends the TextBox control and provides a slider control functionality that allows you to use the slider to select a number from a predefined range.
SlideShowExtender	Extends the Image control to provide a slideshow functionality.
TabContainer	Represents a simple TabStrip control.
TabPanel	Represents a panel in the TabContainer control. Contains the "view" of each tab.
TextBoxWatermarkExtender	Extends the TextBox control. Enables you to provide a watermark for your textboxes, which allows you to overlay text over the textbox that disappears when you enter a value.
ToggleButtonExtender	Extends the Button control. Provides the functionality for a button to toggle between text values or images when clicked.
ToolkitScriptManager	Extends the ScriptManager control and provides a more efficient caching model targeted at the ASP.NET AJAX Control Toolkit functionality.
UpdatePanelAnimationExtender	Extends the UpdatePanel control. Enables you to specify animations that will execute inside of your UpdatePanels.
ValidatorCalloutExtender	Extends the ASP.NET Validator controls and provides a callout description box when a user entry is invalid.

Again, this Toolkit is designed mainly to save you some development effort and time while providing your users with a very rich user experience. In the next section, you examine an example of a page that uses a few controls in the ASP.NET AJAX Control Toolkit.

Using Controls in the ASP.NET AJAX Control Toolkit

Although it is not practical to demonstrate how to use every control in the ASP.NET AJAX Control Toolkit, this section demonstrates how to use a key subset of the following controls:

- ▶ Accordion and AccordionPane
- ▶ CalendarExtender
- ▶ CascadingDropDown
- ▶ CollapsiblePanelExtender
- ▶ ConfirmButtonExtender
- ▶ DragPanelExtender
- ▶ DropDownExtender
- ▶ FilteredTextBoxExtender
- ▶ HoverMenuExtender
- ▶ TextBoxWatermarkExtender

Configuring Visual Studio to Use the Toolkit

You can easily use Visual Studio to help you build applications that leverage the ASP.NET AJAX Control Toolkit. Other than the new suite of controls that you will have available, there isn't much difference in using the ASP.NET AJAX Control Toolkit controls from using the standard ASP.NET controls. The ASP.NET AJAX Control Toolkit is not something that you install, but rather something that you can download and reference in your projects.

Before you can use the ASP.NET AJAX Control Toolkit, you must first set a reference to the appropriate DLL files in Visual Studio. Because a number of controls will be added to your toolbox, you should consider creating a new tab in your toolbox for the new controls. In the following examples, the new tab is named "AJAX Toolkit."

After you have the new tab, you need to set a reference to the AjaxControlToolkit.dll file, which can be downloaded from the following site: http://www.asp.net/ajax/. You can set the reference to the AjaxControlToolkit.dll file by first selecting the AJAX Toolkit tab from the Visual Studio toolbox and then clicking Choose Items. You then need to browse to the directory that contains the AjaxControlToolkit.dll file (this is the location where you unzipped it to), as illustrated in Figure 7.1. Note that the AjaxControlToolkit.dll provides the extensions in the form of extra controls to the ASP.NET AJAX Framework that ship with the .NET 3.5 Framework.

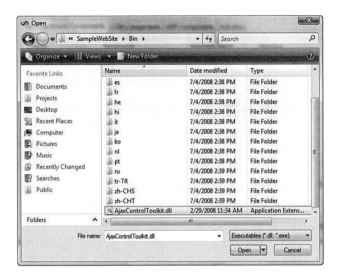

FIGURE 7.1   Setting a reference to AjaxControlToolkit.dll.

After your reference has been set to the ASP.NET AJAX Control Toolkit, you will notice a number of new controls that have been added to the toolbox. Figure 7.2 shows an example of the new toolbox items.

In the next few sections of the chapter, you learn how to use a few of the controls that are included with the ASP.NET AJAX Control Toolkit. These are meant to give you an idea of the capabilities of each control as well as to give you a few springboard projects that you can immediately begin to use in your applications.

The Accordion and AccordionPane Controls

The Accordion and AccordionPane controls are used in conjunction with each other. The basic idea behind these controls is to provide you with a set of collapsible panels, which can be expanded only one at a time. For example, this could be a menu of items with details about each item; however, you only want your users to view the details of one item at a time.

Listing 7.1 shows a page that displays four paragraphs of Lorum Ipsum (http://www.lipsum. com)...but only one paragraph at a time using the Accordion and AccordionPane controls.

FIGURE 7.2   The ASP.NET AJAX controls in the Visual Studio toolbox.

LISTING 7.1   Accordion.aspx

```
<%@ Page Language="C#" %>

<%@ Register Assembly="AjaxControlToolkit" Namespace="AjaxControlToolkit"
TagPrefix="cc1" %>

<!DOCTYPE html PUBLIC "-//W3C//DTD XHTML 1.0 Transitional//EN"
➥"http://www.w3.org/TR/xhtml1/DTD/xhtml1-transitional.dtd">

<script runat="server">

</script>

<html xmlns="http://www.w3.org/1999/xhtml">
<head runat="server">
    <title>Untitled Page</title>
    <script type="text/javascript">

      function pageLoad() {
      }
```

LISTING 7.1   Continued

```
    </script>
<style type="text/css">
    .header
    {
        background-color: Gray;
        color: White;
        font-weight: bold;
        border: thin;
        border-color: Black;
        cursor:hand;
    }
</style>
</head>
<body>
    <form id="form1" runat="server">
    <div>
        <asp:ScriptManager ID="ScriptManager1" runat="server" />
        <center>
            <h2>Lorum Ipsum Paragraphs</h2>
        </center>
        <cc1:Accordion ID="Accordion1"
            runat="server"
            AutoSize="None"
            FadeTransitions="True"
            SelectedIndex="0"
            HeaderCssClass="header">
            <Panes>
                <cc1:AccordionPane runat="server" ID="AccordionPane1">
                    <Header>Open Paragraph 1</Header>
                    <Content>
<i>Lorem ipsum dolor sit amet, consectetuer adipiscing elit. Vivamus adipiscing,
erat quis convallis dapibus, tellus turpis sodales quam, vitae ultricies enim felis
sit amet ligula. Proin quis elit. Nam quis ligula sed purus adipiscing fermentum.
Quisque vitae sapien non nunc egestas porta. Nunc eget lorem. Cras in tortor ac
nisi malesuada cursus. Nulla placerat hendrerit elit. Sed a sapien. Nulla justo
velit, vestibulum vel, gravida nec, varius in, risus. Phasellus vel eros. Nam enim.
Morbi sed augue. Nulla et dui quis leo faucibus viverra. Vestibulum neque. Ut
molestie nisl vel mi. Maecenas pharetra nulla ut velit. Maecenas adipiscing vene-
natis lacus. Etiam tincidunt consectetuer sem. Ut accumsan leo sed diam. Nullam
convallis euismod magna. </i>

<br /><br />
                    </Content>
                </cc1:AccordionPane>
                <cc1:AccordionPane runat="server" ID="AccordionPane2">
```

```
                  <Header>Open Paragraph 2</Header>
                  <Content>
<i>Integer ornare. Cras pretium consequat sapien. Sed non tortor. Integer tellus
ligula, ullamcorper sed, scelerisque ut, condimentum id, sapien. Aenean sed velit
et odio tristique bibendum. Donec at mauris. Sed mauris. Morbi eros. Ut eu nisi.
Proin molestie quam id diam. Ut eget velit ut dui ornare sollicitudin. Quisque fau-
cibus, turpis vel viverra congue, tortor felis porta nisl, a feugiat nibh mauris
eget felis. Proin fermentum, odio vel vulputate dictum, eros enim tempor eros, nec
semper risus nisl sed nulla. Vestibulum pharetra, sem sed consectetuer vulputate,
sapien nulla malesuada lorem, sed elementum dui felis eget quam. Mauris suscipit
rhoncus libero. Fusce erat dui, eleifend eget, tincidunt quis, gravida et, nulla.
Aenean non sapien vitae eros adipiscing eleifend. </i>

<br /><br />
                  </Content>
              </cc1:AccordionPane>
              <cc1:AccordionPane runat="server" ID="AccordionPane3">
                  <Header>Open Paragraph 3</Header>
                  <Content>
<i>Nam mollis, pede vitae dignissim sollicitudin, dui augue eleifend elit, at
vulputate turpis urna vitae turpis. Pellentesque gravida porta est. Mauris sit amet
leo. Fusce eu sapien. Nullam purus dui, dictum nec, lobortis vitae, pretium quis,
sapien. Duis congue faucibus velit. Donec tempor. Sed et urna sit amet ante dapibus
congue. Suspendisse id orci. Mauris vitae lacus eget purus cursus accumsan. In enim
eros, facilisis quis, egestas vitae, consectetuer et, purus. Nam quis sem. Sus-
pendisse imperdiet urna tristique mi. Nullam vestibulum bibendum neque. Morbi con-
sequat luctus felis. Donec posuere risus a justo.</i>

<br /><br />
                  </Content>
              </cc1:AccordionPane>
              <cc1:AccordionPane runat="server" ID="AccordionPane4">
                  <Header>Open Paragraph 4</Header>
                  <Content>
<i>Mauris convallis sem ultricies felis tempus scelerisque. Nunc vitae lorem. Prae-
sent tortor libero, rhoncus id, aliquam ultrices, molestie vel, turpis. Nunc mol-
lis. Phasellus dui ante, congue nec, accumsan sit amet, laoreet sit amet, felis. In
hac habitasse platea dictumst. Donec lacus leo, feugiat sed, varius ac, lobortis
eu, ipsum. Nullam sagittis, velit a rutrum congue, pede mi condimentum lorem, quis
pulvinar odio arcu ut nulla. Sed euismod, urna vitae elementum viverra, orci dolor
facilisis mi, elementum faucibus leo odio nec dui. Curabitur mollis enim ut mi.
Nullam ut purus. Aenean a nulla in mi tincidunt dictum. Nam ante enim, consequat
sit amet, posuere et, mattis ut, justo. Sed accumsan ornare ligula. Mauris eros
ante, dapibus at, lobortis a, consectetuer auctor, elit. Nunc interdum. Nam sit
amet dui. Maecenas tristique neque nec velit. </i>
```

LISTING 7.1   Continued

```
<br /><br />
                    </Content>
                </cc1:AccordionPane>
            </Panes>
        </cc1:Accordion>
    </div>
    </form>
</body>
</html>
```

To use the Accordion and AccordionPane, you need to understand their relationship. The Accordion is the root control in that it provides the accordion-like functionality and the AccordionPane control is where you will place the text that the user sees. The Accordion has the following properties that have been configured in this example:

► **AutoSize**—Automatically sizes the control to fit the contents to the screen

► **FadeTransitions**—Provides a nice DHTML-like fade-in fade-out when the panes are changing

► **SelectedIndex**—Displays the index of the selected item when the control loads

► **HeaderCssClass**—Styles the header in each AccordionPane control

After you have configured an Accordion control on your page, you can then begin to add AccordionPane controls and associate them with the Accordion control. Each AccordionPane control has two required subsections that you must configure:

► **Header**—The header of the AccordionPane control. This is what the user clicks to activate each AccordionPane.

► **Content**—The content that is displayed to the user when an AccordionPane is expanded.

In this example, four paragraphs of Lorem Ipsum are displayed, each in their own AccordionPane control. Figure 7.3 displays the rendered page.

The CalendarExtender Control

The CalendarExtender control is a nice control that you can use to display calendars to your users so that they can easily select a date. You will find yourself using this control more and more as it is easy to use and very functional. One of the issues with the "out-of-the-box" ASP.NET Calendar control is that it isn't really that good if you want to provide your users with a popup calendar so that they can select a date and move on. The CalendarExtender is also one of the easiest controls to learn to use because it simply extends a native ASP.NET control to provide date selection functionality via a popup calendar to your users.

Listing 7.2 illustrates a page with a TextBox control and a CalendarExtender to allow you to easily select a date from a popup calendar.

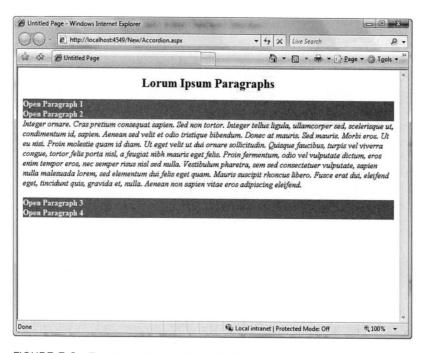

FIGURE 7.3   The Accordion and AccordionPane controls.

LISTING 7.2   CalendarExtender.aspx

```
<%@ Page Language="C#" %>


<%@ Register Assembly="AjaxControlToolkit"
Namespace="AjaxControlToolkit" TagPrefix="cc1" %>

<!DOCTYPE html PUBLIC "-//W3C//DTD XHTML 1.0 Transitional//EN"
➥"http://www.w3.org/TR/xhtml1/DTD/xhtml1-transitional.dtd">

<script runat="server">

</script>

<html xmlns="http://www.w3.org/1999/xhtml">
<head runat="server">
    <title>Untitled Page</title>
    <script type="text/javascript">

      function pageLoad() {
      }

    </script>
</head>
<body>
    <form id="form1" runat="server">
```

LISTING 7.2   Continued

```
    <div>
        <asp:ScriptManager ID="ScriptManager1" runat="server" />
        Select a Date:
        <asp:TextBox ID="TextBox1"
            runat="server"
            ReadOnly="true"></asp:TextBox>
        <cc1:CalendarExtender
            ID="CalendarExtender1"
            runat="server"
            TargetControlID="TextBox1">
        </cc1:CalendarExtender>
    </div>
    </form>
</body>
</html>
```

After creating the TextBox that you would like to use with a CalendarExtender on your form, you need to drop a CalendarExtender on your page and then associate it with the TextBox, setting the TargetControlID property of the CalendarExtender control to the ID of the TextBox control. After associating the CalendarExtender control with the TextBox, you can activate it by simply clicking on the TextBox control. When you click on the TextBox, the calendar drops down below the TextBox and you can then select a date, which will be placed back in the TextBox. In Listing 7.2, the TextBox is marked as Read Only, but that is not required.

> **NOTE**
>
> Note that you aren't required to place the controls in the ASP.NET AJAX Control Toolkit next to the associated ASP.NET control. However, your code will be more maintainable if you do keep the associated controls near each other. In Listing 7.2, the TextBox and CalendarExtender controls are right next to each other.
>
> Figure 7.4 illustrates the CalendarExtender control that was created with Listing 7.2.

The CollapsiblePanelExtender Control

The CollapsiblePanelExtender control is similar to the Accordion control. One limitation (or "feature") of the Accordion control is that you can only expand one panel section at a time; when you expand a new section, the section that you are currently viewing closes and the new section opens. The CollapsiblePanelExtender control allows you to expand and collapse every panel individually so that you can view all of the content at one time.

The CollapsiblePanelExtender is typically used to create very robust, dynamic menus and navigation structures for your application, but it can also be used to display content to your users. Listing 7.3 illustrates the CollapsiblePanelExtender control as it is being used to show and hide content on the page.

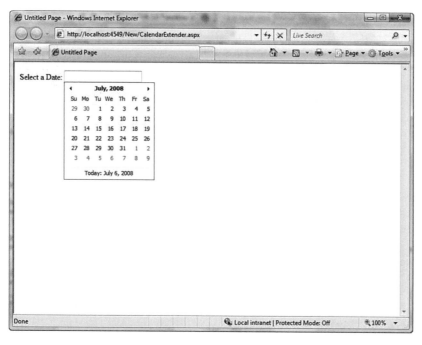

FIGURE 7.4   CalendarExtender control.

LISTING 7.3   CollapsePanel.aspx

```
<%@ Page Language="C#" %>

<%@ Register Assembly="AjaxControlToolkit" Namespace="AjaxControlToolkit"
➡TagPrefix="cc1" %>

<!DOCTYPE html PUBLIC "-//W3C//DTD XHTML 1.0 Transitional//EN"
➡"http://www.w3.org/TR/xhtml1/DTD/xhtml1-transitional.dtd">

<script runat="server">

</script>

<html xmlns="http://www.w3.org/1999/xhtml">
<head runat="server">
    <title>Untitled Page</title>
    <script type="text/javascript">

      function pageLoad() {
      }

    </script>
```

LISTING 7.3   Continued

```
<style type="text/css">
    .panelHeader
    {
            cursor:hand;
            background-color:Gray;
            color:White;
    }
</style>
</head>
<body>
    <form id="form1" runat="server">
    <div style="text-align:center;">
        <asp:ScriptManager ID="ScriptManager1" runat="server" />
        <center>
            <h2>Lorum Ipsum Paragraphs</h2>

            <br />
            <asp:Panel ID="pnl1Header" runat="server" CssClass="panelHeader">
                Show first Lorem Ipsum paragraph
            </asp:Panel>
            <asp:Panel ID="pnl1Content" runat="server">
                <i>Lorem ipsum dolor sit amet, consectetuer adipiscing elit. Viva-
mus adipiscing, erat quis convallis dapibus, tellus turpis sodales quam, vitae
ultricies enim felis sit amet ligula. Proin quis elit. Nam quis ligula sed purus
adipiscing fermentum. Quisque vitae sapien non nunc egestas porta. Nunc eget lorem.
Cras in tortor ac nisi malesuada cursus. Nulla placerat hendrerit elit. Sed a
sapien. Nulla justo velit, vestibulum vel, gravida nec, varius in, risus. Phasellus
vel eros. Nam enim. Morbi sed augue. Nulla et dui quis leo faucibus viverra.
Vestibulum neque. Ut molestie nisl vel mi. Maecenas pharetra nulla ut velit. Maece-
nas adipiscing venenatis lacus. Etiam tincidunt consectetuer sem. Ut accumsan leo
sed diam. Nullam convallis euismod magna.</i>
            </asp:Panel>

            <cc1:CollapsiblePanelExtender
                ID="CollapsiblePanelExtender1"
                runat="server"
                TargetControlID="pnl1Content"
                CollapseControlID="pnl1Header"
                ExpandControlID="pnl1Header"
                Collapsed="true">
            </cc1:CollapsiblePanelExtender>

            <br />
```

```
<asp:Panel ID="pnl2Header" runat="server" CssClass="panelHeader">
    Show second Lorem Ipsum paragraph
</asp:Panel>
<asp:Panel ID="pnl2Content" runat="server">
    <i>Integer ornare. Cras pretium consequat sapien. Sed non tortor.
Integer tellus ligula, ullamcorper sed, scelerisque ut, condimentum id, sapien.
Aenean sed velit et odio tristique bibendum. Donec at mauris. Sed mauris. Morbi
eros. Ut eu nisi. Proin molestie quam id diam. Ut eget velit ut dui ornare solici-
tudin. Quisque faucibus, turpis vel viverra congue, tortor felis porta nisl, a feu-
giat nibh mauris eget felis. Proin fermentum, odio vel vulputate dictum, eros enim
tempor eros, nec semper risus nisl sed nulla. Vestibulum pharetra, sem sed con-
sectetuer vulputate, sapien nulla malesuada lorem, sed elementum dui felis eget
quam. Mauris suscipit rhoncus libero. Fusce erat dui, eleifend eget, tincidunt
quis, gravida et, nulla. Aenean non sapien vitae eros adipiscing eleifend. </i>
</asp:Panel>
<cc1:CollapsiblePanelExtender
    ID="CollapsiblePanelExtender2"
    runat="server"
    TargetControlID="pnl2Content"
    CollapseControlID="pnl2Header"
    ExpandControlID="pnl2Header"
    Collapsed="true">
</cc1:CollapsiblePanelExtender>


<br />


<asp:Panel ID="pnl3Header" runat="server" CssClass="panelHeader">
    Show third Lorem Ipsum paragraph
</asp:Panel>
<asp:Panel ID="pnl3Content" runat="server">
    <i>Nam mollis, pede vitae dignissim sollicitudin, dui augue
eleifend elit, at vulputate turpis urna vitae turpis. Pellentesque gravida porta
est. Mauris sit amet leo. Fusce eu sapien. Nullam purus dui, dictum nec, lobortis
vitae, pretium quis, sapien. Duis congue faucibus velit. Donec tempor. Sed et urna
sit amet ante dapibus congue. Suspendisse id orci. Mauris vitae lacus eget purus
cursus accumsan. In enim eros, facilisis quis, egestas vitae, consectetuer et,
purus. Nam quis sem. Suspendisse imperdiet urna tristique mi. Nullam vestibulum
bibendum neque. Morbi consequat luctus felis. Donec posuere risus a justo.</i>
</asp:Panel>
<cc1:CollapsiblePanelExtender
    ID="CollapsiblePanelExtender3"
    runat="server"
    TargetControlID="pnl3Content"
    CollapseControlID="pnl3Header"
    ExpandControlID="pnl3Header"
    Collapsed="true">
```

LISTING 7.3   Continued

```
            </cc1:CollapsiblePanelExtender>
            <br />
        </center>
    </div>
    </form>
</body>
</html>
```

For each set of text that you want to associate with a CollapsiblePanelExtender control, you need to define two ASP.NET Panel controls: one for the header and one for the content. This is illustrated in Figure 7.5.

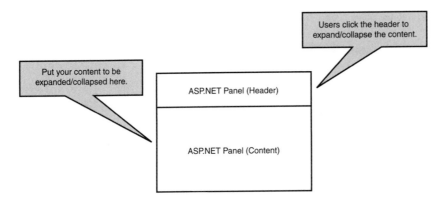

FIGURE 7.5   Creating two ASP.NET Panels for each CollapsiblePanelExtender.

After creating your two panels, you can then associate them with a CollapsiblePanelExtender control. Note that you need to create a CollapsiblePanelExtender for each set of panels to which you want to apply the expand/collapse functionality.

Given the following code excerpt from Listing 7.3, you can see how easy it is to associate the CollapsiblePanelExtender control with the Header and Content ASP.NET Panel controls.

```
<asp:Panel ID="pnl1Header" runat="server" CssClass="panelHeader">
    Show first Lorem Ipsum paragraph
</asp:Panel>
<asp:Panel ID="pnl1Content" runat="server">
    <i>Lorem ipsum dolor sit amet...(content omitted for brevity)
</asp:Panel>

<cc1:CollapsiblePanelExtender
    ID="CollapsiblePanelExtender1"
    runat="server"
    TargetControlID="pnl1Content"
```

```
         CollapseControlID="pnl1Header"
         ExpandControlID="pnl1Header"
         Collapsed="true">
     </cc1:CollapsiblePanelExtender>
```

The ASP.NET Panel that is being used for the header is named "pnl1Header" and the Panel that is being used to display the content is named "pnl1Content." Directly below the ASP.NET Header and Content Panels is the associated CollapsiblePanelExtender control. The following list describes each of the properties that have been configured in the CollapsiblePanelExtender control:

▶ **TargetControlID**—The content you want expanded and collapsed. This is sometimes confusing as the TargetControlID is usually the control that the user directly interacts with; however, with the CollapsiblePanelExtender control, it refers to the content itself.

▶ **CollapseControlID**—The ID of the ASP.NET Panel control that will be used to collapse the content (defined by the TargetControlID property) when the user clicks the text.

▶ **ExpandControlID**—The ID of the ASP.NET Panel control that will be used to expand the content (defined by the TargetControlID property) when the user clicks the text.

Figure 7.6 illustrates three CollapsiblePanelExtender controls, two of which are expanded to show the differences between it and the Accordion controls.

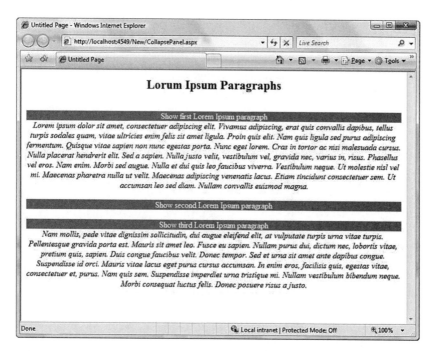

FIGURE 7.6   CollapsiblePanelExtender controls.

The ConfirmButtonExtender Control

The ConfirmButtonExtender control is another one of the more useful controls in the
ASP.NET AJAX Control Toolkit. At its core, it provides a way for you to prompt your users
before the page posts back to the server. By default, this happens by using a JavaScript
Alert box, but can also leverage a ModalPopupExtender control from the ASP.NET AJAX
Control Toolkit.

Listing 7.4 illustrates using the ConfirmButtonExtender to display a JavaScript alert to the
user and the ModalPopupExtender is discussed later in this chapter.

LISTING 7.4   ConfirmButton.aspx

```
<%@ Page Language="C#" %>

<%@ Register Assembly="AjaxControlToolkit" Namespace="AjaxControlToolkit"
➥TagPre fix="cc1" %>

<!DOCTYPE html PUBLIC "-//W3C//DTD XHTML 1.0 Transitional//EN"
➥"http://www.w3.org/TR/xhtml1/DTD/xhtml1-transitional.dtd">

<script runat="server">

</script>

<html xmlns="http://www.w3.org/1999/xhtml">
<head id="Head1" runat="server">
    <title>Untitled Page</title>
    <script type="text/javascript">

      function pageLoad() {
      }

    </script>
</head>
<body>
    <form id="form1" runat="server">
    <div>
        <asp:ScriptManager ID="ScriptManager1" runat="server" />
        <table>
            <tr>
                <td colspan="2">Please enter your information below</td>
            </tr>
            <tr>
                <td colspan=2><hr /></td>
            </tr>
```

```
        <tr>
            <td>Name:</td>
            <td>
                <asp:TextBox ID="txtName" runat="server"></asp:TextBox></td>
        </tr>
        <tr>
            <td>Phone Number:</td>
            <td>
                <asp:TextBox ID="txtPhone" runat="server"></asp:TextBox></td>
        </tr>
        <tr>
            <td></td>
            <td>
                <asp:Button ID="cmdSubmit"
                    runat="server"
                    Text="Submit" />
                <cc1:ConfirmButtonExtender
                    ID="ConfirmButtonExtender1"
                    runat="server"
                    TargetControlID="cmdSubmit"
                    ConfirmText="Are you sure?">
                </cc1:ConfirmButtonExtender>
            </td>
        </tr>
    </table>
  </form>
</body>
</html>
```

In Listing 7.4, a form requests a user's name and phone number; the user can enter this information and then click the Submit button. A ConfirmButtonExtender control associated with the Submit button has the following properties configured:

▸ **TargetControlID**—The ID of the Submit button for which you want to display a message to the user when they click it

▸ **ConfirmText**—The text that you want to display to the user when the JavaScript alert is displayed

In its simplest form, this is all that is required to configure the ConfirmButtonExtender control. Figure 7.7 illustrates the page with the popup that is displayed.

In an example that is covered later in this chapter, you learn how to use the ConfirmButtonExtender control together with a ModalPopupExtender control to provide a very rich user experience with your modal popups.

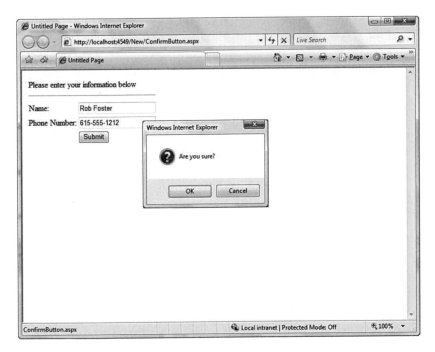

FIGURE 7.7   ConfirmButtonExtender example.

The DragPanelExtender Control

The DragPanelExtender control is a fun control to use because it allows you to provide drag-and-drop functionality to your applications. It is similar to the other panel extenders in that it extends the ASP.NET Panel control. You just need to define the Panel control that is the container for your content and configure the DragPanelExtender, and you instantly have a Panel control that can be dragged around the screen and dropped into a new location on the page.

Listing 7.5 illustrates an ASP.NET page that has a Panel control and a DragPanelExtender control, which allows you to drag and drop the Panel to a new location on the page.

LISTING 7.5   DragPanel.aspx

```
<%@ Page Language="C#" %>

<%@ Register Assembly="AjaxControlToolkit" Namespace="AjaxControlToolkit"
➥TagPrefix="cc1" %>

<!DOCTYPE html PUBLIC "-//W3C//DTD XHTML 1.0 Transitional//EN"
➥"http://www.w3.org/TR/xhtml1/DTD/xhtml1-transitional.dtd">

<script runat="server">
```

```
</script>

<html xmlns="http://www.w3.org/1999/xhtml">
<head runat="server">
    <title>Untitled Page</title>
    <script type="text/javascript">

      function pageLoad() {
      }

    </script>
</head>
<body>
    <form id="form1" runat="server">
    <div>
        <asp:ScriptManager ID="ScriptManager1" runat="server" />

        <asp:Panel runat="server" ID="dragPanel">
            <asp:Panel ID="pnlHeader" runat="server">DRAG ME</asp:Panel>
            <asp:Panel ID="pnlContent" runat="server">
            this is some text in the panel...
            </asp:Panel>
        </asp:Panel>

        <cc1:DragPanelExtender
            ID="DragPanelExtender1"
            runat="server"
            TargetControlID="dragPanel"
            DragHandleID="pnlHeader"
            Enabled="True">
        </cc1:DragPanelExtender>

    </div>
    </form>
</body>
</html>
```

As you can see by Listing 7.5, an ASP.NET Panel control is defined that contains two child panels: pnlHeader and pnlContent. It isn't required that you create a section for the header and content; however, after you associate the Panel controls with the DragPanelExtender control, it is nice to have a header and content area because you can use the header as the handle that the user will use to click and drag the panel around the screen.

The DragPanelExtender control is configured with the following properties:

▶ **TargetControlID**—The ID of the Panel in which you would like to provide drag-and-drop functionality.

▶ **DragHandleID**—The ID of the Panel in which you would like the user to click to initiate the drag. This can be the same value as the TargetControlID, but in this example, it is a child panel to illustrate that you can separate the panels into header and content sections.

The DragPanelExtender control is one of the more difficult controls to illustrate as a figure in a book. However, to gain an idea of what this might look like, Figure 7.8 shows the rendered page created by the code defined in Listing 7.5.

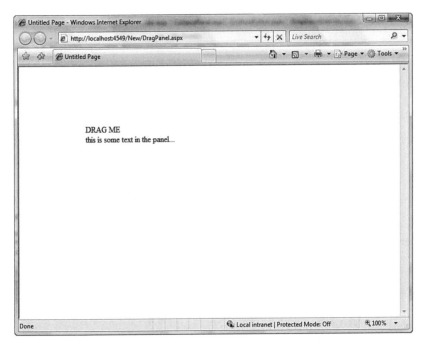

FIGURE 7.8   DragPanelExtender example.

The DropDownExtender Control

The DropDownExtender control provides you with a "SharePoint-like" dropdown functionality for your applications. When you are viewing items in a list in SharePoint or WSS, you can hover over specific fields in the list and a dropdown box appears. When you click the dropdown box, it expands and provides you with a context-sensitive menu to perform a specific task against the specific list item. The DropDownExtender control helps you provide this same type of functionality to your ASP.NET applications quickly and easily.

Listing 7.6 illustrates the use of a DropDownExtender control to extend the functionality of an ASP.NET Label control and provide a dropdown menu to select a favorite color.

LISTING 7.6   DropDownExtender.aspx

```
<%@ Page Language="C#" %>


<%@ Register Assembly="AjaxControlToolkit" Namespace="AjaxControlToolkit"
➥TagPrefix="cc1" %>

<!DOCTYPE html PUBLIC "-//W3C//DTD XHTML 1.0 Transitional//EN"
➥"http://www.w3.org/TR/xhtml1/DTD/xhtml1-transitional.dtd">

<script runat="server">

    protected void linkButton_Click(object sender, EventArgs e)
    {
        Label2.Text = "You selected " + ((LinkButton)sender).Text;
    }
</script>

<html xmlns="http://www.w3.org/1999/xhtml">
<head runat="server">
    <title>Untitled Page</title>
    <script type="text/javascript">

      function pageLoad() {
      }

    </script>
</head>
<body>
    <form id="form1" runat="server">
    <div>
        <asp:ScriptManager ID="ScriptManager1" runat="server" />
        <table style="width:350px;border:solid, thin, black;">
            <tr>
                <td><asp:Label ID="Label1" runat="server">Select your favorite
➥color     </asp:Label></td>
                <td align="right"><asp:Label ID="Label2" runat="server">
➥</asp:Label></td>
            </tr>
        </table>
        <asp:Panel ID="pnlDropdown" runat="server" BackColor="LightGray">
            <asp:LinkButton ID="LinkButton1"
                runat="server"
                Text="Red"
                onclick="linkButton_Click">
```

LISTING 7.6   Continued

```
            </asp:LinkButton>
            <br />
            <asp:LinkButton ID="LinkButton2"
                runat="server"
                Text="Yellow"
                onclick="linkButton_Click">
            </asp:LinkButton>
            <br />
            <asp:LinkButton ID="LinkButton3"
                runat="server"
                Text="Blue"
                onclick="linkButton_Click">
            </asp:LinkButton>
            <br />
        </asp:Panel>
        <cc1:DropDownExtender
            ID="DropDownExtender1"
            runat="server"
            TargetControlID="Label1"
            DropDownControlID="pnlDropdown">
        </cc1:DropDownExtender>
    </div>
    </form>
</body>
</html>
```

The DropDownExtender control in this example is extending the functionality of an ASP.NET Label control named Label1. You must define only one thing before you can use the DropDownExtender control: the format and items in the dropdown itself. You can easily do this by using an ASP.NET Panel control, which is named pnlDropdown in Listing 7.6.

The pnlDropdown Panel control contains several link buttons that all point to the same event handler for the onClick event: linkButton_Click. When a LinkButton is clicked, it raises the server-side linkButton_Click event, which simply sets the value of another Label control on the page to display the color that you selected in the dropdown menu.

After you have your dropdown menu defined, you can drag a DropDownExtender control onto your page and begin to configure it to extend the Label control. In Listing 7.6, the DropDownExtender control, named DropDownExtender1, defines the following properties:

- ▶ **TargetControlID**—The ID of the Label control that you want to display the drop-down control

- ▶ **DropDownControlID**—The ID of the ASP.NET Panel control (or any container control) that defines the layout of your dropdown

Figure 7.9 illustrates the DropDownExtender control and how it looks when you hover over a label and click to display the dropdown menu (notice that a color has already been selected and is being displayed in the label to the right of the dropdown).

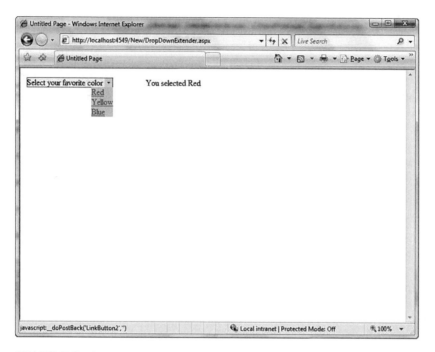

FIGURE 7.9   DropDownExtender example.

The FilteredTextBoxExtender Control

The FilteredTextBoxExtender control allows you to provide a specific "filter" to the contents of your Textbox controls to ensure that the user can only enter a specific set or pattern of characters. You can easily do this by writing a little JavaScript code to do the same thing, but with the FilteredTextBoxExtender, you don't have to write any JavaScript to apply filtering to your ASP.NET TextBox controls.

Listing 7.7 illustrates two FilteredTextBoxExtender controls that are used to limit the input of two TextBox controls.

LISTING 7.7   FilteredTextBoxes.aspx

```
<%@ Page Language="C#" %>


<%@ Register Assembly="AjaxControlToolkit" Namespace="AjaxControlToolkit"
➥TagPrefix="cc1" %>
```

LISTING 7.7   Continued

```
<!DOCTYPE html PUBLIC "-//W3C//DTD XHTML 1.0 Transitional//EN"
➡"http://www.w3.org/TR/xhtml1/DTD/xhtml1-transitional.dtd">

<script runat="server">

</script>

<html xmlns="http://www.w3.org/1999/xhtml">
<head runat="server">
    <title>Untitled Page</title>
    <script type="text/javascript">

      function pageLoad() {
      }

    </script>
</head>
<body>
    <form id="form1" runat="server">
    <div>
        <asp:ScriptManager ID="ScriptManager1" runat="server" />
        <table>
            <tr>
                <td>Name:</td>
                <td>
                    <asp:TextBox ID="TextBox1" runat="server"></asp:TextBox>
                    <cc1:FilteredTextBoxExtender
                        ID="FilteredTextBoxExtender1"
                        runat="server"
                        TargetControlID="TextBox1"
                        FilterType="UppercaseLetters">
                    </cc1:FilteredTextBoxExtender>
                </td>
            </tr>
            <tr>
                <td>Number of years service:</td>
                <td>
                    <asp:TextBox ID="TextBox2" runat="server"></asp:TextBox>
                    <cc1:FilteredTextBoxExtender
                        ID="FilteredTextBoxExtender2"
                        runat="server"
                        TargetControlID="TextBox2"
                        FilterType="Numbers">
                    </cc1:FilteredTextBoxExtender>
                </td>
            </tr>
```

```
            <tr>
                <td></td>
                <td>
                    <asp:Button ID="Button1" runat="server" Text="Submit" /></td>
                </tr>
            </table>
        </div>
        </form>
</body>
</html>
```

In Listing 7.7, you can see that there are two TextBoxes defined: one to accept a name and one to accept the number of years of service. Out of the box, you can configure the FilteredTextBoxExtender control to filter for uppercase characters, lowercase characters, and numbers. You can also specify valid and invalid characters that the filter can be used to compare against. In this example, only uppercase characters and numbers are being filtered for each respective TextBox control.

You can configure the FilteredTextBoxExtender control by setting the following properties:

- **TargetControlID**—The ID of the TextBox control with which you would like to associate the FilteredTextBoxExtender control.

- **FilterType**—The type of filter that will be applied to the TextBox. Possible values are uppercase characters, lowercase characters, numbers, and custom. If you use a custom filter, you must define any valid or invalid characters by setting the ValidChars and InvalidChars properties.

Figure 7.10 illustrates the page that is rendered by Listing 7.7.

The HoverMenuExtender Control

The HoverMenuExtender control allows you to display an ASP.NET Panel control when you hover over an item on the page to display more information about that particular item. This is one of the standard functionalities that you see with AJAX-enabled sites and is a quick way to provide a lot of information to your users about items on the page without having a lot of clutter. Listing 7.8 illustrates using the HoverMenuExtender control to extend the functionality of an ASP.NET Label control.

LISTING 7.8   HoverMenu.aspx

```
<%@ Page Language="C#" %>


<%@ Register Assembly="AjaxControlToolkit"
Namespace="AjaxControlToolkit" TagPrefix="cc1" %>

<!DOCTYPE html PUBLIC "-//W3C//DTD XHTML 1.0 Transitional//EN"
➡"http://www.w3.org/TR/xhtml1/DTD/xhtml1-transitional.dtd">
```

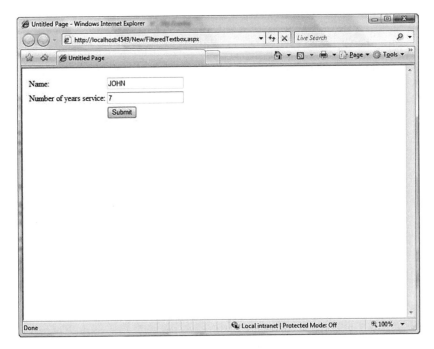

FIGURE 7.10   FilteredTextbox.aspx.

LISTING 7.8   Continued

```
<script runat="server">

</script>

<html xmlns="http://www.w3.org/1999/xhtml">
<head runat="server">
    <title>Untitled Page</title>
    <script type="text/javascript">

      function pageLoad() {
      }

    </script>
        <style type="text/css">
        .hoverBackground
        {
                background-color:Gray;
                filter:alpha(opacity=70);
                opacity:0.7;
        }
        .hoverPopup
```

```
        {
                background-color:#ffffff;
                width:500px;
        }
        .hoverHeader
        {
            font-family: Calibri, Verdana;
            font-weight: bold;
            vertical-align: middle;
            padding-left: 3px;
            height: 24px;
            cursor: hand;
            color: #636973;
            background-image: url(./Images/SilverBarBackground.jpg);
            border-top: solid 2px #636973;
            border-left: solid 2px #636973;
            border-right: solid 2px #636973;
        }
        .hoverContent
        {
            border: solid 2px #636973;
            padding: 5px;
        }
    </style>

</head>
<body>
    <form id="form1" runat="server">
    <div>
        <asp:ScriptManager ID="ScriptManager1" runat="server" />
        <asp:Label ID="Label1" runat="server" Text="">Hover over me to learn
➥more</asp:Label>
        <cc1:HoverMenuExtender
            ID="HoverMenuExtender1"
            runat="server"
            TargetControlID="Label1"
            PopupControlID="pnlHoverMenu"
            PopupPosition="Bottom">
        </cc1:HoverMenuExtender>

        <asp:Panel ID="pnlHoverMenu" runat="server" CssClass="hoverPopup">
            <asp:Panel ID="pnlHeader" runat="server" CssClass="hoverHeader">
                Here is some information
            </asp:Panel>

            <asp:Panel ID="pnlContent" runat="server" CssClass="hoverContent">
```

LISTING 7.8   Continued

```
                Lorem ipsum dolor sit amet, consectetuer adipiscing elit. Vivamus
adipiscing, erat quis convallis dapibus, tellus turpis sodales quam, vitae
ultricies enim felis sit amet ligula. Proin quis elit. Nam quis ligula sed purus
adipiscing fermentum. Quisque vitae sapien non nunc egestas porta. Nunc eget lorem.
Cras in tortor ac nisi malesuada cursus. Nulla placerat hendrerit elit. Sed a
sapien. Nulla justo velit, vestibulum vel, gravida nec, varius in, risus. Phasellus
vel eros. Nam enim. Morbi sed augue. Nulla et dui quis leo faucibus viverra.
Vestibulum neque. Ut molestie nisl vel mi. Maecenas pharetra nulla ut velit. Maece-
nas adipiscing venenatis lacus. Etiam tincidunt consectetuer sem. Ut accumsan leo
sed diam. Nullam convallis euismod magna.
            </asp:Panel>
        </asp:Panel>
    </div>
    </form>
</body>
</html>
```

You need to define only two items before you can use the HoverMenuExtender control: an item that you will use to display information to the user and a container that will be used to display details to the user. In this example, an ASP.NET Label control is used as the base item and an ASP.NET Panel control is used to display the details information when the user hovers over the Label control.

After you have defined your base item and details container, you can drop a HoverMenuExtender control on your page and begin to configure the following properties:

- **TargetControlID**—The base control that forces the details to be displayed when the user hovers over the control.

- **PopupControlID**—The control that contains the details information that will be displayed when the user hovers over the control that is defined by the TargetControlID property.

- **PopupPosition**—The position that you want the popup menu to display against the control defined by the TargetControlID property. Valid values are Bottom, Center, Left, Right, and Top.

Figure 7.11 illustrates the page that is rendered by the code in Listing 7.8 and shows the HoverMenuExtender displayed on the page.

The TextBoxWatermarkExtender Control

You can use the TextBoxWatermarkExtender control to provide a watermark for your ASP.NET TextBox controls. This means that you can have your textboxes display a message while the Text property of the textbox is actually empty. This allows you to define more explicit instructions as to what the user needs to enter into the textbox itself. Listing 7.9 illustrates a page that contains two ASP.NET textboxes that have watermarks assigned to them.

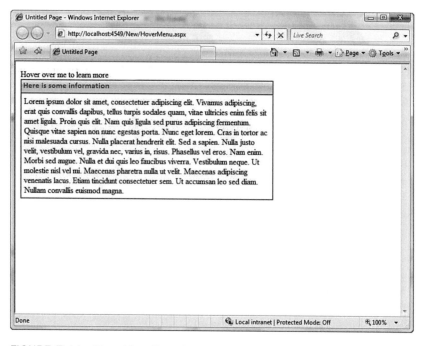

FIGURE 7.11   HoverMenuExtender example.

LISTING 7.9   TextboxWatermark.aspx

```
<%@ Page Language="C#" %>


<%@ Register Assembly="AjaxControlToolkit" Namespace="AjaxControlToolkit"
➥TagPrefix="cc1" %>

<!DOCTYPE html PUBLIC "-//W3C//DTD XHTML 1.0 Transitional//EN"
➥"http://www.w3.org/TR/xhtml1/DTD/xhtml1-transitional.dtd">

<script runat="server">

</script>

<html xmlns="http://www.w3.org/1999/xhtml">
<head runat="server">
    <title>Untitled Page</title>
    <script type="text/javascript">

    function pageLoad() {
    }
```

LISTING 7.9   Continued

```
    </script>
    <style type="text/css">
        .watermarkColor
        {
            color:Gray;
        }
    </style>
</head>
<body>
    <form id="form1" runat="server">
    <div>
        <asp:ScriptManager ID="ScriptManager1" runat="server" />
        <table>
            <tr>
                <td>Name:</td>
                <td>
                    <asp:TextBox ID="TextBox1" runat="server"></asp:TextBox>
                    <cc1:TextBoxWatermarkExtender
                        ID="TextBoxWatermarkExtender1"
                        runat="server"
                        WatermarkCssClass="watermarkColor"
                        WatermarkText="Enter your name"
                        TargetControlID="TextBox1">
                    </cc1:TextBoxWatermarkExtender>
                </td>
            </tr>
            <tr>
                <td>Requested Vacation Date:</td>
                <td>
                    <asp:TextBox ID="TextBox2" runat="server"></asp:TextBox>
                    <cc1:TextBoxWatermarkExtender
                        ID="TextBoxWatermarkExtender2"
                        runat="server"
                        TargetControlID="TextBox2"
                        WatermarkCssClass="watermarkColor"
                        WatermarkText="Enter a date">
                    </cc1:TextBoxWatermarkExtender>
                </td>
            </tr>
            <tr>
                <td></td>
                <td>
                    <asp:Button ID="Button1" runat="server" Text="Submit" /></td>
            </tr>
```

```
            </table>
        </div>
        </form>
</body>
</html>
```

Using the TextBoxWatermarkExtender control is very simple; all that you need is a TextBox control and you can immediately use the TextBoxWatermarkExtender control to provide a watermark for the textbox. You need to configure the following properties for the TextBoxWatermarkExtender control:

▶ **TargetControlID**—The ID of the TextBox control that you want to associate with the TextBoxWatermarkExtender control

▶ **WatermarkText**—The text that you want to display as a watermark

▶ **WatermarkCSSClass**—An optional property, but if you have a CSS Class defined to style your watermark (the example in Listing 7.9 simply sets the color of the watermark's text to gray), you can specify that style in this property

Figure 7.12 illustrates the rendered page that is defined by Listing 7.9 with the watermarked TextBox controls.

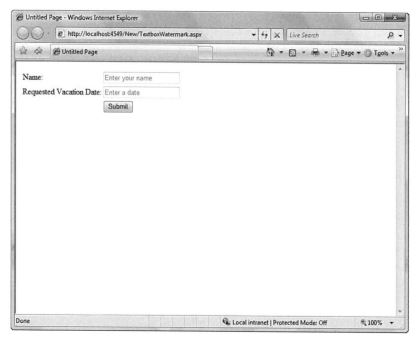

FIGURE 7.12   TextBoxWatermarkExtender example.

ASP.NET AJAX Control Toolkit: A Practical Example

In this example, you learn how to use the ModalPopupExtender control along with other ASP.NET controls to show a modal window and collect information from the user.

The first thing you should do before you start coding with the ASP.NET AJAX Control Toolkit is decide how you want your page to look. This can be as simple as defining a stylesheet or as complex as a custom theme for your application. The example in this section uses the stylesheet in Listing 7.10 to define the look and feel of the items that will be displayed on the page.

LISTING 7.10   The Styles

```
<style type="text/css">
    body
    {
        font-family: Calibri, Verdana;
    }
    a:link, a:visited, a:active
    {
        color: #000066;
        text-decoration: none;
    }
    .modalBackground
    {
        background-color:Gray;
        filter:alpha(opacity=70);
        opacity:0.7;
    }
    .modalPopup
    {
        background-color:#ffffff;
        width:600px;
    }
    .modalHeader
    {
        font-family: Calibri, Verdana;
        font-weight: bold;
        vertical-align: middle;
        padding-left: 3px;
        height: 24px;
        cursor: hand;
        color: #636973;
        background-image: url(./Images/SilverBarBackground.jpg);
        border-top: solid 2px #636973;
        border-left: solid 2px #636973;
```

```
        border-right: solid 2px #636973;
    }
    .modalHeaderImageButton
    {
        border: 0px;
        padding: 0px;
        margin-left: 0px;
        margin-bottom: 0px;
        margin-right: 3px;
        margin-top: 4px;
    }
    .modalContent
    {
        border: solid 2px #636973;
        padding: 5px;
    }
    .notThere
    {
        display: none;
    }
    .ActionButton
    {
        border: #8B8B8B 1px solid;
        font-size: 8pt;
        color: #000066;
        background-color: #F9F9F9;
        height:18;
        filter: progid:DXImageTransform.Microsoft.Gradient(gradientType=0,
➡startColorStr=#F9F9F9,endColorStr=#B5B5B5);
        cursor: hand;
        width: 100px;
    }
    .sideBar
    {
        padding-right: 15px;
    }
</style>
```

Although self-explanatory, the stylesheet will define how your users perceive your application. It doesn't matter how "cool" the ASP.NET AJAX Control Toolkit is; if your page isn't
visually appealing, your users will not care. In this stylesheet, the colors have a grayscale
tone to them, which is optimized for how the screenshots are printed on the page (in
black and white). However, the page looks decent in full color if you are going for a metal-
lic look and feel.

Before the code is explored, you should look at the page and the modal dialog boxes that get displayed in Figures 7.13 through 7.16.

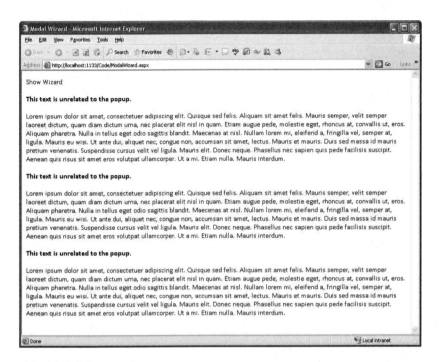

FIGURE 7.13   Sample web page.

In Figure 7.13, you will notice a sample web page (note that the paragraph content was generated from http://www.lipsum.com). This web page has some content displayed and a link in the upper-left corner of the page called Show Wizard. When a user clicks on the Show Wizard link, a modal dialog box is displayed with an ASP.NET Wizard control that is used to collect information from the user.

In Figures 7.14, 7.15, and 7.16, you can see the results of walking through the wizard. Notice how the original page (in the background) is grayed out a bit to place full focus on the modal window. Also, any link, button, and so on (basically, anything a user can click on the page) becomes disabled while the modal window is displayed.

You can add the ASP.NET AJAX Control Toolkit to your project by performing the following steps:

1. Right-click your toolbox and then click the Choose Items option.

2. Click the Browse button and browse to the location where the ASP.NET AJAXControlToolkit.dll file is located.

3. Select the DLL, click the Open button, and then click OK to add the controls to the toolbox.

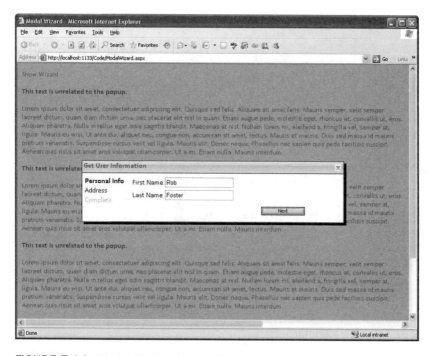

FIGURE 7.14   Modal window: Wizard Step 1.

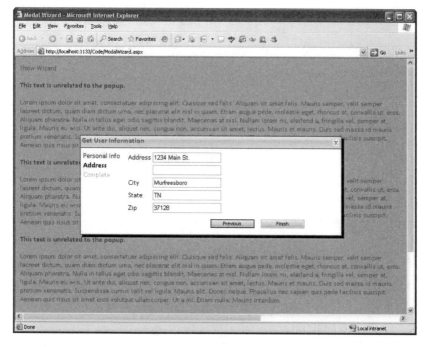

FIGURE 7.15   Modal window: Wizard Step 2.

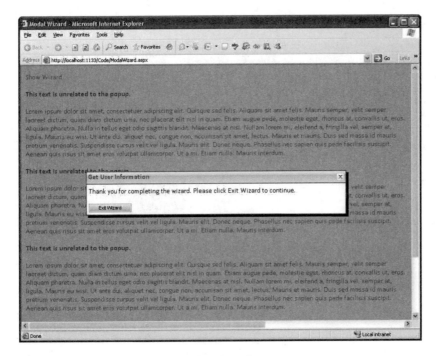

FIGURE 7.16   Modal window: Wizard Step 3.

Figure 7.17 illustrates the toolbox with the ASP.NET AJAX Control Toolkit added.

Now, take a look at how simple this type of functionality is to implement in the code in Listing 7.11.

LISTING 7.11   ModalWizard.aspx

```
<%@ Page Language="C#" AutoEventWireup="true" CodeFile="ModalWizard.aspx.cs"
➥Inherits="ModalWizard" %>
<%@ Register Assembly="AjaxControlToolkit" Namespace="AjaxControlToolkit"
➥TagPrefix="ajax" %>

<!DOCTYPE html PUBLIC "-//W3C//DTD XHTML 1.0 Transitional//EN"
➥"http://www.w3.org/TR/xhtml1/DTD/xhtml1-transitional.dtd">

<html xmlns="http://www.w3.org/1999/xhtml" >
<head id="Head1" runat="server">
    <title>Modal Wizard</title>
<style type="text/css">
    body
    {
```

FIGURE 7.17   ASP.NET AJAX Control Toolkit added to the toolbox.

```
    font-family: Calibri, Verdana;
}
a:link, a:visited, a:active
{
    color: #000066;
    text-decoration: none;
}
.modalBackground
{
    background-color:Gray;
    filter:alpha(opacity=70);
    opacity:0.7;
}
.modalPopup
{
    background-color:#ffffff;
    width:600px;
}
```

LISTING 7.11   Continued

```
.modalHeader
{
    font-family: Calibri, Verdana;
    font-weight: bold;
    vertical-align: middle;
    padding-left: 3px;
    height: 24px;
    cursor: hand;
    color: #636973;
    background-image: url(./Images/SilverBarBackground.jpg);
    border-top: solid 2px #636973;
    border-left: solid 2px #636973;
    border-right: solid 2px #636973;
}
.modalHeaderImageButton
{
    border: 0px;
    padding: 0px;
    margin-left: 0px;
    margin-bottom: 0px;
    margin-right: 3px;
    margin-top: 4px;
}
.modalContent
{
    border: solid 2px #636973;
    padding: 5px;
}
.notThere
{
    display: none;
}
.ActionButton
{
    border: #8B8B8B 1px solid;
    font-size: 8pt;
    color: #000066;
    background-color: #F9F9F9;
    height:18;
    filter: progid:DXImageTransform.Microsoft.Gradient(gradientType=0,
startColorStr=#F9F9F9,endColorStr=#B5B5B5);
    cursor: hand;
    width: 100px;
}
.sideBar
{
```

```
        padding-right: 15px;
    }
</style>
</head>
<body>
    <form id="form1" runat="server">
        <ajax:ToolkitScriptManager ID="scriptManager" Runat="server" />
        <asp:LinkButton ID="lnkShowWizard" runat="server" Text="Show Wizard" />
        <p><strong>This text is unrelated to the popup.</strong></p>
        <p>Lorem ipsum dolor sit amet, consectetuer adipiscing elit. Quisque sed
felis. Aliquam sit amet felis. Mauris semper, velit semper laoreet dictum, quam
diam dictum urna, nec placerat elit nisl in quam. Etiam augue pede, molestie eget,
rhoncus at, convallis ut, eros. Aliquam pharetra. Nulla in tellus eget odio sagit-
tis blandit. Maecenas at nisl. Nullam lorem mi, eleifend a, fringilla vel, semper
at, ligula. Mauris eu wisi. Ut ante dui, aliquet nec, congue non, accumsan sit
amet, lectus. Mauris et mauris. Duis sed massa id mauris pretium venenatis. Sus-
pendisse cursus velit vel ligula. Mauris elit. Donec neque. Phasellus nec sapien
quis pede facilisis suscipit. Aenean quis risus sit amet eros volutpat ullamcorper.
Ut a mi. Etiam nulla. Mauris interdum.</p>
        <p><strong>This text is unrelated to the popup.</strong></p>
        <p>Lorem ipsum dolor sit amet, consectetuer adipiscing elit. Quisque sed
felis. Aliquam sit amet felis. Mauris semper, velit semper laoreet dictum, quam
diam dictum urna, nec placerat elit nisl in quam. Etiam augue pede, molestie eget,
rhoncus at, convallis ut, eros. Aliquam pharetra. Nulla in tellus eget odio sagit-
tis blandit. Maecenas at nisl. Nullam lorem mi, eleifend a, fringilla vel, semper
at, ligula. Mauris eu wisi. Ut ante dui, aliquet nec, congue non, accumsan sit
amet, lectus. Mauris et mauris. Duis sed massa id mauris pretium venenatis. Sus-
pendisse cursus velit vel ligula. Mauris elit. Donec neque. Phasellus nec sapien
quis pede facilisis suscipit. Aenean quis risus sit amet eros volutpat ullamcorper.
Ut a mi. Etiam nulla. Mauris interdum.</p>
        <p><strong>This text is unrelated to the popup.</strong></p>
        <p>Lorem ipsum dolor sit amet, consectetuer adipiscing elit. Quisque sed
felis. Aliquam sit amet felis. Mauris semper, velit semper laoreet dictum, quam
diam dictum urna, nec placerat elit nisl in quam. Etiam augue pede, molestie eget,
rhoncus at, convallis ut, eros. Aliquam pharetra. Nulla in tellus eget odio sagit-
tis blandit. Maecenas at nisl. Nullam lorem mi, eleifend a, fringilla vel, semper
at, ligula. Mauris eu wisi. Ut ante dui, aliquet nec, congue non, accumsan sit
amet, lectus. Mauris et mauris. Duis sed massa id mauris pretium venenatis. Sus-
pendisse cursus velit vel ligula. Mauris elit. Donec neque. Phasellus nec sapien
quis pede facilisis suscipit. Aenean quis risus sit amet eros volutpat ullamcorper.
Ut a mi. Etiam nulla. Mauris interdum.</p>
        <asp:Panel ID="Popup1" runat="server" CssClass="modalPopup"
➥style="display: none;">
            <asp:Panel ID="PopupHeader1" runat="server" CssClass="modalHeader">
                <span style="float: left;">
                    Get User Information
```

LISTING 7.11   Continued

```
                    </span>
                    <span style="float: right;">
                        <asp:ImageButton ID="PopupClose1" runat="server"
 ImageUrl="~/Images/SilverCloseButton.jpg"
                            Height="17" Width="18" CssClass="modalHeaderImageButton" />
                    </span>
                </asp:Panel>
                <asp:Panel ID="PopupContent1" runat="server" CssClass="modalContent">
                    <asp:UpdatePanel ID="UpdateContent1" runat="server">
                    <ContentTemplate>
                        <asp:Wizard ID="Wizard1" runat="server"
                            SideBarStyle-VerticalAlign="Top"
                            SideBarStyle-CssClass="sideBar">
                            <CancelButtonStyle CssClass="ActionButton" />
                            <NavigationButtonStyle CssClass="ActionButton" />
                            <WizardSteps>
                                <asp:WizardStep runat="server" Title="Personal Info">
                                    <table>
                                    <tr>
                                        <td>First Name</td>
                                        <td>
<asp:TextBox ID="FirstName" runat="server" /></td>
                                        <td>
                                            <asp:RequiredFieldValidator runat="server"
                                                ControlToValidate="FirstName"
                                                Text="Please enter a first name." />
                                        </td>
                                    </tr>
                                    <tr>
                                        <td>Last Name</td>
                                        <td><asp:TextBox ID="LastName" runat="server"
➥/></td>
                                        <td>
                                            <asp:RequiredFieldValidator
ID="RequiredFieldValidator1" runat="server"
                                                ControlToValidate="LastName"
                                                Text="Please enter a last name." />
                                        </td>
                                    </tr>
                                    </table>
                                </asp:WizardStep>
                                <asp:WizardStep runat="server" Title="Address">
                                    <table>
                                    <tr>
                                        <td>Address</td>
```

```
                                    <td><asp:TextBox ID="Address1" runat="server"
➡/></td>
                                    <td>
                                        <asp:RequiredFieldValidator
 ID="RequiredFieldValidator2" runat="server"
                                            ControlToValidate="Address1"
                                            Text="Please enter
a street address." />
                                    </td>
                                </tr>
                                <tr>
                                    <td></td>
                                    <td><asp:TextBox ID="Address2" runat="server"
➡/></td>
                                    <td></td>
                                </tr>
                                <tr>
                                    <td>City</td>
                                    <td><asp:TextBox ID="City" runat="server" /></td>
                                    <td>
                                        <asp:RequiredFieldValidator
 ID="RequiredFieldValidator3" runat="server"
                                            ControlToValidate="City"
                                            Text="Please enter a city." />
                                    </td>
                                </tr>
                                <tr>
                                    <td>State</td>
                                    <td><asp:TextBox ID="State" runat="server"
➡MaxLength="2" /></td>
                                    <td>
                                        <asp:RequiredFieldValidator
 ID="RequiredFieldValidator4" runat="server"
                                            ControlToValidate="State"
                                            Text="Please enter a state." />
                                    </td>
                                </tr>
                                <tr>
                                    <td>Zip</td>
                                    <td><asp:TextBox ID="Zip" runat="server"
➡MaxLength="5" /></td>
                                    <td>
                                        <asp:RequiredFieldValidator
 ID="RequiredFieldValidator5" runat="server"
                                            ControlToValidate="Zip"
                                            Text="Please enter a zip." />
                                    </td>
```

7

LISTING 7.11   Continued

```
                                            </tr>
                                        </table>
                                    </asp:WizardStep>
                                    <asp:WizardStep runat="server" Title="Complete"
➡StepType="Complete">
                                        Thank you for completing the wizard.
Please click Exit Wizard to continue.
                                        <br />
                                        <asp:Button CssClass="ActionButton" ID="OkButton"
➡runat="server" OnClientClick="document.getElementById('PopupOk1').click();
➡return false;" Text="Exit Wizard" />
                                    </asp:WizardStep>
                                </WizardSteps>
                            </asp:Wizard>

                        </ContentTemplate>
                        </asp:UpdatePanel>
                        <asp:Button CssClass="notThere" ID="PopupOk1" runat="server"
➡Text="OK" OnClick="Ok_ButtonClick" />
                    </asp:Panel>
                </asp:Panel>
                <ajax:ModalPopupExtender ID="PopupExtender" runat="server"
                    TargetControlID="lnkShowWizard"
                    PopupControlID="Popup1"
                    BackgroundCssClass="modalBackground"
                    OkControlID="PopupOk1"
                    CancelControlID="PopupClose1"
                    DropShadow="true"
                    PopupDragHandleControlID="PopupHeader1" Drag="true"
                    OnOkScript="__doPostBack('PopupOk1', '');" />
            </form>
        </body>
        </html>
```

The code is very simple because the majority of it is standard ASP.NET! Actually, if you focus on the last control defined on the page, the ModalPopupExtender, you will notice that it is the only control on the page used in the ASP.NET AJAX Control Toolkit.

To dig a little deeper in this example, the page really contains three things: the page content itself, a panel that contains an ASP.NET Wizard control that will be displayed as the modal popup window, and a ModalPopupExtender control.

In its simplest form, the ModalPopupExtender control defines four things:

- ▶ The control that causes the modal popup to be displayed

- ▶ The panel that is used as the modal popup

- ▶ The stylesheet classes that define the look and feel of the modal window

- ▶ The buttons that are used to close the modal dialog box (in this example, the OK and Cancel buttons)

Isn't that easy? Using these controls enables you to capitalize on the investment you've made in your current skills as well as save you a lot of time and effort in manually coding for the same functionality.

Fortunately, Visual Studio isn't the only tool you can use to take advantage of the ASP.NET AJAX Control Toolkit. In the next section, you learn how to utilize the ASP.NET AJAX Control Toolkit with Microsoft Expression Web.

Using the ASP.NET AJAX Control Toolkit with Microsoft Expression Web

Microsoft has recently released the Expression suite of tools that are targeted at creating very rich, interactive user experiences. These tools are largely targeted at graphics designers and web page designers/developers so that a set of tools (other than Visual Studio) can be used to focus on the user experience and not the code (C#/VB.NET, etc.) behind the user interface itself.

The Microsoft Expression suite of tools is separated into the following four core tools:

- ▶ **Expression Web**—Web page designer that is focused on creating HTML/ASP.NET pages

- ▶ **Expression Design**—Graphics design tool for creating and modifying graphics files

- ▶ **Expression Blend**—Windows Presentation Foundation designer tool for creating user interfaces for WFP windows-based applications

- ▶ **Expression Media**—Media asset manager tool that is used to organize your rich media files

Many times, especially with larger teams, you might have a team that is dedicated to designing user interfaces with Microsoft Expression Web (or maybe it's you wearing all of those hats on your team), which is separate from your core development team that uses Visual Studio 2008. Although it is a great web design tool, Expression Web isn't as intuitive to use in the ASP.NET AJAX Control Toolkit as it is in Visual Studio 2008. In this section, you learn how to configure Expression Web to use the ASP.NET AJAX Control Toolkit.

Configuring Expression Web for the ASP.NET AJAX Control Toolkit

You must do two things to use the ASP.NET AJAX Control Toolkit with Microsoft Expression Web:

- ▶ Register the Toolkit in the Global Assembly Cache (GAC).

- ▶ Modify the Web.Config file to recognize the Toolkit and provide IntelliSense in the code.

It is very easy to register the Toolkit in the GAC. Just follow these steps:

1. Open the Microsoft .NET Framework 2.0 Configuration, which is located in the Administrative Tools (see Figure 7.18).

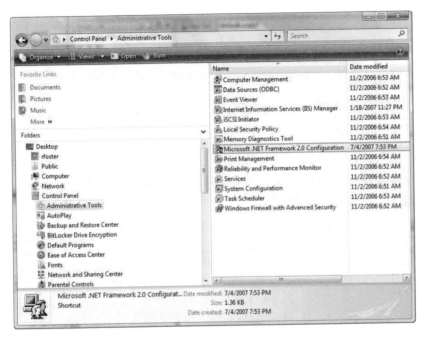

FIGURE 7.18   Microsoft .NET Framework 2.0 Configuration.

2. Click on the Manage Assembly Cache link, as shown in Figure 7.19.

3. In the Assembly Cache window that appears, click on the Add an Assembly to the Assembly Cache link to add a new assembly to the GAC, as shown in Figure 7.20.

   When you click on the Add an Assembly to the Assembly Cache link, you see an Open File dialog box that allows you to select the assembly that you want to add. In Figure 7.21, the AjaxControlToolkit.dll file is being selected.

4. Click the Open button to install the selected assembly to the GAC.

> **NOTE**
>
> Note that the AjaxControlToolkit.dll file has already been assigned a strong name, which means that you can simply download the DLL and install it in the GAC.

After the assembly has been installed to the GAC, you need to display its properties window to reference the installed version and the public key token. These values will be referenced by your web site's Web.Config file. The assembly properties are illustrated in Figure 7.22.

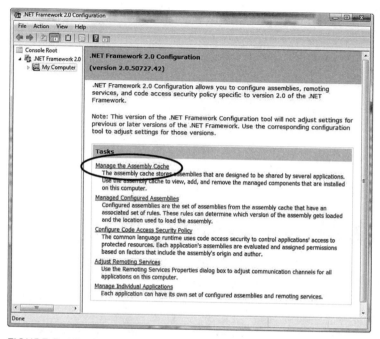

FIGURE 7.19   Managing Assemblies in the GAC.

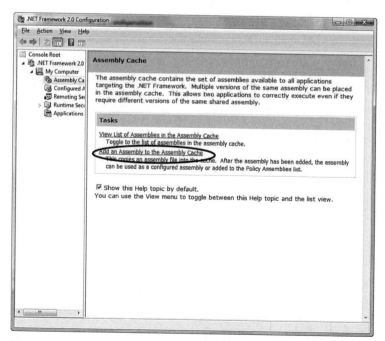

FIGURE 7.20   Adding an Assembly to the GAC.

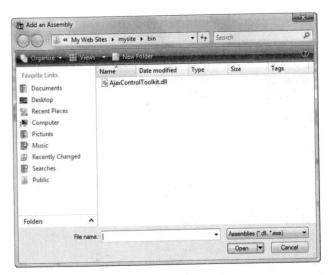

FIGURE 7.21 Selecting the AjaxControlToolkit.dll assembly.

> **NOTE**
>
> Note that your public key token and version could be different from what's shown in Figure 7.22. When you install the Toolkit to your local GAC, please verify these values because your Web.Config values need to match these property values exactly or the AJAX Control Toolkit will not work correctly with Expression Web.

After you have registered the AjaxControlToolkit.dll file in the GAC on your development machine, you can now begin to configure Expression Web. When you create a web site, you need to either create a custom Web.Config file or modify the existing one to reference the ASP.NET AJAX Control Toolkit.

The following code is an example of the modified Web.Config file:

```
<?xml version="1.0"?>
<configuration>
    <appSettings/>
    <connectionStrings/>
    <system.web>
        <pages>
          <controls>
            <add tagPrefix="asp" namespace="System.Web.UI"
➥assembly="System.Web.Extensions, Version=1.0.61025.0, Culture=neutral,
➥PublicKeyToken=31bf3856ad364e35"/>
            <add tagPrefix="ajax" namespace="AjaxControlToolkit"
➥assembly="AjaxControlToolkit, Version=1.0.10920.32880, Culture=neutral,
➥PublicKeyToken=28f01b0e84b6d53e"/>
```

FIGURE 7.22   The AjaxControlToolkit properties.

```
        </controls>
      </pages>

      <compilation debug="true">
        <assemblies>
         <add assembly="System.Web.Extensions, Version=1.0.61025.0,
➥Culture=neutral, PublicKeyToken=31bf3856ad364e35"/>
           <add assembly="System.Design, Version=2.0.0.0, Culture=neutral,
➥PublicKeyToken=B03F5F7F11D50A3A"/>
           <add assembly="System.Web.Extensions.Design, Version=1.0.61025.0,
➥Culture=neutral, PublicKeyToken=31BF3856AD364E35"/>
           <add assembly="System.Windows.Forms, Version=2.0.0.0, Culture=neutral,
➥PublicKeyToken=B77A5C561934E089"/>
           <add assembly="AjaxControlToolkit, Version=1.0.10920.32880,
➥Culture=neutral, PublicKeyToken=28f01b0e84b6d53e"/>
         </assemblies>
      </compilation>

      <authentication mode="Windows" />

   </system.web>
</configuration>
```

Notice the new sections that define custom <pages> and <assemblies> elements. The Web.Config file is where you need to reference the version number and public key token value that was illustrated in Figure 7.22 because you need to bind to a specific version of the AjaxControlToolkit.dll assembly.

After you create and/or modify the Web.Config file, you must close and restart Expression Web for your changes to take effect. When you reload your project, you will have IntelliSense for the ASP.NET AJAX Control Toolkit, as illustrated by Figure 7.23.

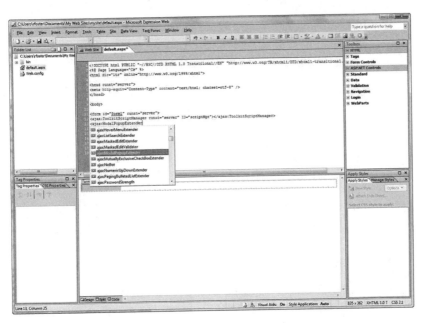

FIGURE 7.23   Expression Web and the ASP.NET AJAX Control Toolkit.

Summary

The ASP.NET AJAX Control Toolkit provides a lot of capabilities that can save you quite a bit of time in your coding efforts. In this chapter, you learned about the available controls in the ASP.NET AJAX Control Toolkit, how to use them to provide a more robust user experience, and how to allow your web designers to capitalize on the Toolkit with Expression Web.

CHAPTER 8

Building an ASP.NET AJAX Extender Control

As you learned in Chapter 7, "Using the ASP.NET AJAX Control Toolkit," ASP.NET AJAX Extender Controls enable you to easily extend the functionality of an existing ASP.NET standard control (such as a TextBox, Button, or Label control). In this section, you learn how to use the Visual Studio 2008 tools to add a control extender to a standard ASP.NET control.

Add ASP.NET Controls

First, you need a page with some controls, which is defined in Listing 8.1.

LISTING 8.1   ASP.NET Controls

```
<%@ Page Language="C#" AutoEventWireup="true"
CodeBehind="ExtenderDemo.aspx.cs" Inherits="TestHar-
ness.ExtenderDemo" %>

<%@ Register assembly="AjaxControlToolkit"
namespace="AjaxControlToolkit" tagprefix="cc1" %>

<!DOCTYPE html PUBLIC "-//W3C//DTD XHTML 1.0 Transi-
tional//EN"
 "http://www.w3.org/TR/xhtml1/DTD/xhtml1-
transitional.dtd">

<html xmlns="http://www.w3.org/1999/xhtml" >
<head runat="server">
    <title>Untitled Page</title>
    <script type="text/javascript">
```

LISTING 8.1   Continued

```
        function pageLoad() {
        }

    </script>
</head>
<body>
    <form id="form1" runat="server">
    <div>
        <asp:ScriptManager ID="ScriptManager1" runat="server" />
        <table>
            <tr>
                <td>Enter a number: </td>
                <td>
                    <asp:TextBox ID="TextBox1" runat="server"></asp:TextBox>
                </td>
            </tr>
            <tr>
                <td colspan="2" align="right">
                    <asp:Button ID="Button1" runat="server" onclick="Button1_Click"
Text="Button" />
                </td>

            </tr>
        </table>
    </div>
    </form>
</body>
</html>
```

As you can see in Listing 8.1, a TextBox and a Button control have been defined on the page so that a user can enter a number into the TextBox and submit it to the server.

In the traditional web world, if you want to limit what the user can enter into the TextBox to only numbers, you have to write some (and sometimes a lot of) JavaScript to accomplish this task. Lucky for us as developers, there is a nice little control extender in the ASP.NET AJAX Control Toolkit, called the FilteredTextBoxExtender, that can accomplish this task without writing any JavaScript!

> **NOTE**
>
> Before you can add this extender control to your page, you first must set a reference to the AjaxControlToolkit.dll file, which is the ASP.NET AJAX Control Toolkit.

Visual Studio 2008 has a few new features that make adding control extenders to your ASP.NET Controls very easy. Figure 8.1 illustrates the fly-out menu that is available on each control in the Visual Studio Page Designer.

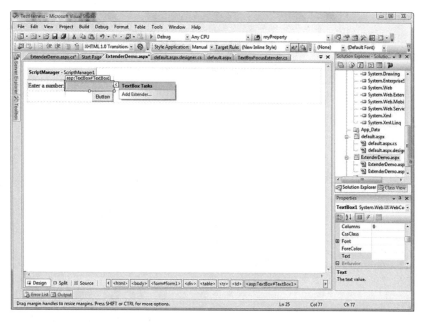

FIGURE 8.1   Adding an Extender control.

When you select a control in the designer, it will have an icon in the top-right corner that, when clicked, displays a menu which allows you to add a control extender to the selected control.

When you click on the Add Extender link, you are presented with a modal dialog, in which you can select an extender for the selected control (see Figure 8.2).

After you select an extender for your control (in this example, FilteredTextboxExtender is selected), Visual Studio automatically associates the extender with your control. The following code excerpt shows the FilteredTextBoxExtender that has been associated with the TextBox on the page.

```
<tr>
    <td>Enter a number: </td>
    <td>
        <asp:TextBox ID="TextBox1" runat="server"></asp:TextBox>
        <cc1:FilteredTextBoxExtender ID="TextBox1_FilteredTextBoxExtender"
            runat="server" Enabled="True" FilterType="Numbers"
TargetControlID="TextBox1">
        </cc1:FilteredTextBoxExtender>
    </td>
</tr>
```

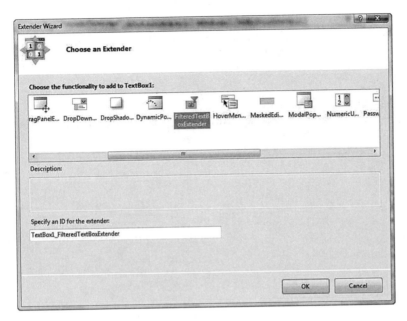

FIGURE 8.2   Select a control extender.

When you look at the properties of your TextBox, you will notice that it now has a new section that has been added called Extenders. This section displays all the properties that have been defined by the extender control, which usually affect the behavior that is applied to your ASP.NET control. Figure 8.3 shows the Extenders section of the Properties window in Visual Studio.

You will notice that the extender control has a property called FilterType, which is set to Numbers. This will automatically set a filter on the TextBox where only numbers can be entered. You can also define valid and invalid characters for the TextBox for more complex filtering.

After you learn how to use the extender controls that are included in the ASP.NET AJAX Control Toolkit, you will begin to see how many hours of writing and testing JavaScript you can save by using them. In the next section, you learn how to build an ASP.NET Extender Control.

How to Build an Extender Control

Building extender controls is quite a simple task, but because you are utilizing a library that automatically generates code for you, it can be a very frustrating experience. In this section, you learn how to build an extender control for a TextBox that changes the style of the TextBox when it has focus. Although you can find similar examples on the Internet as well as on MSDN, this section focuses on explaining why you have to follow some very specific rules when building control extenders so that your first experience with building a control extender will be a positive one.

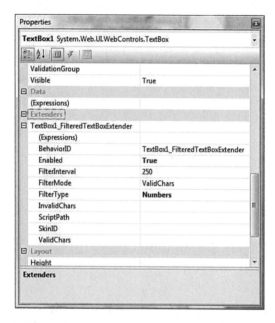

FIGURE 8.3   Extender properties on a TextBox.

One of the first things that you will notice when using Visual Studio 2008 to create an AJAX-enabled extender control is that a project template is available to make the job of setting up the project easy. This project template is called ASP.NET AJAX Server Control Extender, shown in Figure 8.4.

When you create the project and add it to your solution (the examples in this chapter use a project named FocusExtender), you will notice that three files are part of the template:

1. **ClientBehavior1.js**—Used for the JavaScript that will execute behind your control extender. This script will act as the client-side representation of the object defined in the ExtenderControl1.cs file.

2. **ClientBehavior1.resx**—Resource file for your extender control.

3. **ExtenderControl1.cs**—The C# class that defines your extender control.

NOTE

In the example covered throughout this section, the default name of ExtenderControl1.cs will be changed to TextBoxFocusExtender.cs.

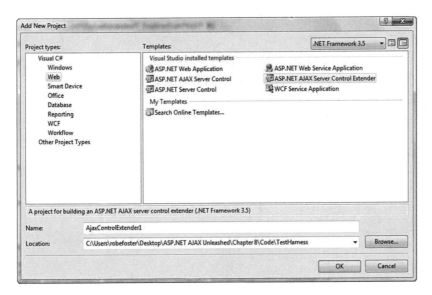

FIGURE 8.4   ASP.NET AJAX Server Control Extender Project.

Server-Side Code

Listing 8.2 is a code example of the TextBoxFocusExtender.cs file that will be used as an example throughout this section.

LISTING 8.2   TextBoxFocusExtender.cs

```
using System;
using System.Collections.Generic;
using System.Configuration;
using System.Linq;
using System.Web;
using System.Web.Security;
using System.Web.UI;
using System.Web.UI.WebControls;
using System.Web.UI.WebControls.WebParts;
using System.Web.UI.HtmlControls;
using System.Xml.Linq;

namespace FocusExtender
{
    [
        TargetControlType(typeof(TextBox))
    ]
    public class TextBoxFocusExtender : ExtenderControl
```

```
    {
        public TextBoxFocusExtender(){}

        private string _focusCSSClass;
        private string _nofocusCSSClass;

        public string FocusCSSClass
        {
            get { return _focusCSSClass; }
            set { _focusCSSClass = value; }
        }
        public string NoFocusCSSClass
        {
            get { return _nofocusCSSClass; }
            set { _nofocusCSSClass = value; }
        }

        protected override IEnumerable<ScriptDescriptor>
                GetScriptDescriptors(System.Web.UI.Control targetControl)
        {
            ScriptBehaviorDescriptor descriptor = new
 ScriptBehaviorDescriptor("FocusExtender.ClientBehavior1",
targetControl.ClientID);
            descriptor.AddProperty("FocusCSSClass", this.FocusCSSClass);
            descriptor.AddProperty("NoFocusCSSClass", this.NoFocusCSSClass);
            yield return descriptor;
        }

        // Generate the script reference
        protected override IEnumerable<ScriptReference>
                GetScriptReferences()
        {
            yield return new ScriptReference(
"FocusExtender.ClientBehavior1.js", this.GetType().Assembly.FullName);
        }
    }
}
```

Starting at the top of the code that defines the class and working down through the code, the first thing you notice is that the class inherits from the ExtenderControl base class. This is a new class in ASP.NET 3.5 that provides the base framework for building control extenders for the ASP.NET controls.

> **NOTE**
>
> Note that the `ExtenderControl` base class is a separate base class than that provid-
> ed by the ASP.NET AJAX Control Toolkit, as the toolkit was released before the .NET 3.5
> Framework and is considered a separate "community-driven" library.

The next thing you should notice is the `TargetControlType` attribute that is used to deco-
rate the class. When you first create the project, this attribute looks like the following
code excerpt:

```
TargetControlType(typeof(Control))
```

Having this attribute means that you can apply your extender for every control that inherits from the Control base class (which is all of them!).

In the code example that is used in this chapter, the extender is limited so that it can only
be applied to a TextBox by using this code:

```
TargetControlType(typeof(TextBox))
```

Now, because the control extender will change how a TextBox looks, it needs to store values
for stylesheet classes that need to get applied when the control either receives or loses focus.
String properties have been defined to hold both values and are named `FocusCSSClass` and
`NoFocusCSSClass`.

> **CAUTION**
>
> It is *very* important to take note of the casing of your property names because you will
> be accessing these properties from client-side JavaScript, and you will run into issues
> if you miss a casing when trying to execute your code.

Up until this point, you have your basic class that inherits from a base class and defines
two properties. The next thing that must be done is to override two methods of the base
class: `GetScriptDescriptors` and `GetScriptReferences`.

The `GetScriptDescriptors` enables you to define any behaviors that need to be converted
into client-side script. In the example in Listing 8.2, since the value of the class applied to
the textbox needs to be changed to the value defined by the `FocusCSSClass` or the
`NoFocusCSSClass` properties, each property must be "pushed" down to the client so that it
can be referenced. This can be accomplished using the `AddProperty` method of the
`ScriptBehaviorDescriptor` object, as done in the following code excerpt from the
example:

LISTING 8.3   Defining the Client-Side Properties

```
ScriptBehaviorDescriptor descriptor = new
ScriptBehaviorDescriptor("FocusExtender.ClientBehavior1",
targetControl.ClientID);
            descriptor.AddProperty("FocusCSSClass", this.FocusCSSClass);
            descriptor.AddProperty("NoFocusCSSClass", this.NoFocusCSSClass);
```

Each AddProperty method accepts a name and a value parameter, which is how the value will be represented in client-side code. Although it isn't required, you should keep these names and their casing the same as was defined in the class to minimize confusion because you may have many properties being pushed to the client.

The GetScriptReferences method simply allows you to define where the JavaScript of your class is defined. This seems trivial, but it is important to note that when your project is compiled, the JavaScript file will be packaged into the assembly so that it can be distributed with the compiled DLL file. (For example, you won't have to distribute your compiled DLL *and* your JavaScript file.)

At its core, this describes the TextBoxFocusExtender.cs class. After you learn how to override the methods previously defined and get some experience with the ExtenderControl base class, creating the C# representation of your control extenders will become seamless.

Client-Side Code

The next file you have to define is the file that contains the JavaScript, or client-side code, for your control extender. This section is probably the most important to understand because it can be the most tedious.

Listing 8.4 defines the ClientBehavior1.js file.

LISTING 8.4   ClientBehavior1.js

```
Type.registerNamespace("FocusExtender");


FocusExtender.ClientBehavior1 = function(element) {
    FocusExtender.ClientBehavior1.initializeBase(this, [element]);

    this._FocusCSSClass = null;
    this._NoFocusCSSClass = null;

}


FocusExtender.ClientBehavior1.prototype = {
    initialize: function() {
        FocusExtender.ClientBehavior1.callBaseMethod(this, 'initialize');
```

LISTING 8.4   Continued

```
        // Add custom initialization here
        $addHandlers(this.get_element(), {'focus': this._onFocus,
'blur': this._onBlur}, this)

    },
    dispose: function() {
        //Add custom dispose actions here
        FocusExtender.ClientBehavior1.callBaseMethod(this, 'dispose');
    },
    _onFocus: function(e) {
        if (this.get_element() && !this.get_element().disabled) {
            this.get_element().className = this._FocusCSSClass;
        }

    },

    _onBlur: function(e) {
        if (this.get_element() && !this.get_element().disabled) {
            this.get_element().className = this._NoFocusCSSClass;
        }
    },

    get_FocusCSSClass : function() {
        return this._FocusCSSClass;
    },

    set_FocusCSSClass : function(value) {
        this._FocusCSSClass = value;
    },

    get_NoFocusCSSClass : function() {
        return this._NofocusCSSClass;
    },

    set_NoFocusCSSClass : function(value) {
        this._NofocusCSSClass = value;
    }
}
FocusExtender.ClientBehavior1.registerClass('FocusExtender.ClientBehavior1',
Sys.UI.Behavior);

if (typeof(Sys) !== 'undefined') Sys.Application.notifyScriptLoaded();
```

Again, starting from the top of the file and working down through the code, the first thing that the JavaScript does is register the namespace "FocusExtender". This registers the server-side namespace that contains the TextBoxFocusExtender class (refer to Listing 8.2). This simply registers the namespace with the client-side code so that classes defined inside the namespace can be referenced in JavaScript.

Next, a function named initializeBase is defined. This function is used to initialize any client-side variables that will be used by the JavaScript. In the TextBoxFocusExtender example, variables are initialized for the FocusCSSClass and the NoFocusCSSClass server-side properties so that they can be stored properly on the client side.

After you initialize the variables that you will be consuming from server-side code, you must then create a JavaScript prototype class of the object being sent from the server to the client. This prototype class is where the client-side logic of your control will live. The very first definition of the prototype is an initialize function, which can be thought of as similar to a C# class constructor method. In the initialize function, you need to set up any event handlers that will be fired by a user interacting with the control that you are extending. In Listing 8.4, event handlers are configured for the onFocus and onBlur events of the associated TextBox. The _onFocus and _onBlur methods that are defined below the initialize function contain the logic that will get executed when a control either receives or loses focus.

Finally, because there are two properties being exposed to the client from the server-side logic (refer to Listing 8.2), you need to create getters and setters for each property. Each getter and setter *must* be named with a prefix of either get_ or set_ and then the name of the property that is exposed to the client (refer to Listing 8.3).

This is quite possibly the most frustrating part of developing control extenders and why it helps to be consistent when naming properties and sending them from the server to the client. One of the benefits of using a library that emits code for you is that it saves you a lot of development time. A disadvantage is that sometimes you must follow certain rules, and specific naming of getters and setters is one of those rules. So what happens if you do have a mismatch with your getters and setters? You will receive a runtime error in the code that is being generated by the library because it will not be able to find the corresponding getter or setter. An example of this error is shown in Figure 8.5.

If you do encounter this message (and it is likely that you will), just take a deep breath and carefully look at how you are exposing your properties on the server side (refer to Listing 8.3), and then verify that you have client-side getters and setters defined for each property with the appropriate prefix (either get_ or set_). After these small details are flushed out, your code should begin to at least begin to execute the event that's being fired. (You are on your own with the logic that you have written inside each event.)

Finally, there are two lines of "cleanup" code in the JavaScript file that first register the code in the behavior file as a behavior, and then fire the notifyScriptLoaded event of the ASP.NET AJAX client-side API.

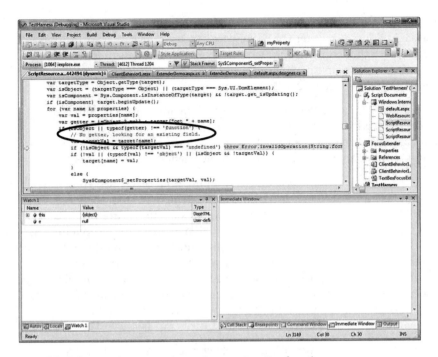

FIGURE 8.5   Runtime error due to incorrect getter function.

After you compile the control extender and add a reference to the assembly, you can then associate it with a TextBox that is defined on your ASP.NET page. Listing 8.5 demonstrates how to associate the TextBoxFocusExtender control with a TextBox on the page.

LISTING 8.5   Default.aspx

```
<%@ Page Language="C#" AutoEventWireup="true"
CodeBehind="default.aspx.cs" Inherits="TestHarness._default" %>

<%@ Register Assembly="FocusExtender" Namespace="FocusExtender" TagPrefix="cc1" %>

<!DOCTYPE html PUBLIC "-//W3C//DTD XHTML 1.0 Transitional//EN"
 "http://www.w3.org/TR/xhtml1/DTD/xhtml1-transitional.dtd">

<html xmlns="http://www.w3.org/1999/xhtml" >
<head runat="server">
    <title>Untitled Page</title>
    <script type="text/javascript">

    function pageLoad() {
    }
```

```
    </script>
    <style type="text/css">
        .ColorYellow
        {
            background-color: Yellow;
        }
        .ColorNormal
        {
            background-color:White;
        }
    </style>
</head>
<body>
    <form id="form1" runat="server">
    <div>
        <asp:ScriptManager ID="ScriptManager1" runat="server" />
        <asp:TextBox ID="TextBox1" runat="server"></asp:TextBox>
<cc1:TextBoxFocusExtender ID="TextBoxFocusExtender1" runat="server"
TargetControlID="TextBox1" FocusCSSClass="ColorYellow" />
    </div>
    </form>
</body>
</html>
```

Because all the logic to toggle the stylesheet class when a control receives and loses focus is wrapped up in the TextBoxFocusExtender control, all that you will be required to do after you associate the TextBoxFocusExtender with a TextBox is define the stylesheet classes that will change the look of the TextBox control and then set the `FocusCSSClass` and `NoFocusCSSClass` properties of the TextBoxFocusExtender control.

Figure 8.6 illustrates the TextBox control as it has focus. (Note that the styles might be lost due to the black-and-white screenshot in the book.)

Summary

In this chapter, you learned about using ASP.NET AJAX Extender Controls in an ASP.NET web page with Visual Studio 2008 by using the FilteredTextBoxExtender, which is a control contained in the ASP.NET AJAX Control Toolkit. After learning how to apply control extenders to standard ASP.NET controls, you learned how to create an extender control as well as many of the "gotchas" that you could encounter when developing your own extender controls.

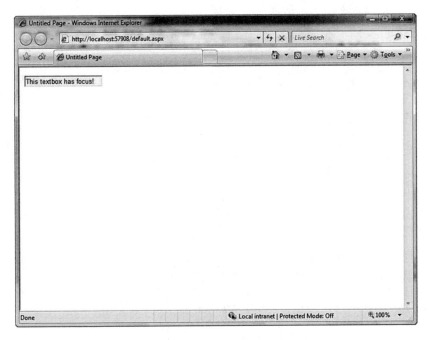

FIGURE 8.6   TextBoxFocusExtender control in an ASP.NET page.

CHAPTER 9

ASP.NET AJAX and SharePoint 2007

SharePoint and AJAX

SharePoint implements quite a few AJAX features, such as the presence indicators that update automatically when users come on and offline (assuming you have an association with Live Communications Server's instant messaging capabilities). Although out of the box, there are AJAX-based features baked into SharePoint—it doesn't natively support ASP.NET AJAX out of the box.

If you are doing your research on this topic, you will see a lot of explanations as to why there is no support for ASP.NET AJAX in SharePoint. It all boils down to the timing of the product releases: SharePoint, ASP.NET AJAX, and the .NET 3.5 Framework. SharePoint 2007 and Windows SharePoint Services (WSS) 3.0 were released to manufacturing roughly one year before .NET 3.5, thus providing some reasonable explanation for the exclusion.

Now, does this mean that you can't utilize what you've learned thus far in this book to implement ASP.NET AJAX SharePoint solutions? Absolutely not! You can indeed use all your ASP.NET AJAX skills that you have acquired to implement solutions in SharePoint 2007 and WSS 3.0. All that you need to do is to configure a few key items in SharePoint/WSS to ensure that the SharePoint runtime knows about the ASP.NET AJAX assemblies.

In this chapter, you learn how to modify the SharePoint/WSS Web.Config file to enable ASP.NET AJAX in SharePoint. You then develop an ASP.NET AJAX-enabled web part that runs in a Windows SharePoint Services Team Site.

Modifying Web.Config

Modifying the SharePoint/WSS Web.Config file to use ASP.NET AJAX and the .NET 3.5 Framework can be very intimidating because there are many things contained in the file. In comparison to a default ASP.NET web site's Web.Config file (out of the box), the SharePoint/WSS Web.Config is easily four times larger in size.

With this size difference in mind, if you take a look at an out of the box ASP.NET Web.Config, there are lots of clues to which sections and settings of the SharePoint/WSS Web.Config file must be changed. (Actually, you can copy directly from the ASP.NET Web.Config file.) Listing 9.1 shows the out of the box ASP.NET 3.5 Web.Config file.

LISTING 9.1   ASP.NET Web.Config File

```
<?xml version="1.0"?>
<configuration>
    <configSections>
        <sectionGroup name="system.web.extensions"
 type="System.Web.Configuration.SystemWebExtensionsSectionGroup,
System.Web.Extensions, Version=3.5.0.0, Culture=neutral,
 PublicKeyToken=31BF3856AD364E35">
        <sectionGroup name="scripting"
 type="System.Web.Configuration.ScriptingSectionGroup,
System.Web.Extensions, Version=3.5.0.0, Culture=neutral,
 PublicKeyToken=31BF3856AD364E35">
        <section name="scriptResourceHandler"
 type="System.Web.Configuration.ScriptingScriptResourceHandlerSection,
System.Web.Extensions, Version=3.5.0.0, Culture=neutral,
 PublicKeyToken=31BF3856AD364E35" requirePermission="false"
 allowDefinition="MachineToApplication"/>
        <sectionGroup name="webServices"
 type="System.Web.Configuration.ScriptingWebServicesSectionGroup,
System.Web.Extensions, Version=3.5.0.0, Culture=neutral,
 PublicKeyToken=31BF3856AD364E35">
        <section name="jsonSerialization"
 type="System.Web.Configuration.ScriptingJsonSerializationSection,
System.Web.Extensions, Version=3.5.0.0, Culture=neutral,
PublicKeyToken=31BF3856AD364E35" requirePermission="false"
 allowDefinition="Everywhere" />
        <section name="profileService"
 type="System.Web.Configuration.ScriptingProfileServiceSection,
System.Web.Extensions, Version=3.5.0.0, Culture=neutral,
 PublicKeyToken=31BF3856AD364E35" requirePermission="false"
 allowDefinition="MachineToApplication" />
        <section name="authenticationService"
 type="System.Web.Configuration.ScriptingAuthenticationServiceSection,
```

```
System.Web.Extensions, Version=3.5.0.0, Culture=neutral,
PublicKeyToken=31BF3856AD364E35" requirePermission="false"
allowDefinition="MachineToApplication" />
        <section name="roleService"
type="System.Web.Configuration.ScriptingRoleServiceSection,
System.Web.Extensions, Version=3.5.0.0, Culture=neutral,
PublicKeyToken=31BF3856AD364E35" requirePermission="false"
allowDefinition="MachineToApplication" />
          </sectionGroup>
        </sectionGroup>
      </sectionGroup>
    </configSections>


    <appSettings/>
    <connectionStrings/>
    <system.web>
        <!—
            Set compilation debug="true" to insert debugging
            symbols into the compiled page. Because this
            affects performance, set this value to true only
            during development.
        —>
        <compilation debug="false">
          <assemblies>
            <add assembly="System.Core, Version=3.5.0.0,
Culture=neutral, PublicKeyToken=B77A5C561934E089"/>
            <add assembly="System.Web.Extensions, Version=3.5.0.0,
Culture=neutral, PublicKeyToken=31BF3856AD364E35"/>
            <add assembly="System.Data.DataSetExtensions,
Version=3.5.0.0, Culture=neutral, PublicKeyToken=B77A5C561934E089"/>
            <add assembly="System.Xml.Linq, Version=3.5.0.0,
Culture=neutral, PublicKeyToken=B77A5C561934E089"/>
          </assemblies>
        </compilation>
        <authentication mode="Windows" />

      <pages>
        <controls>
          <add tagPrefix="asp" namespace="System.Web.UI"
assembly="System.Web.Extensions, Version=3.5.0.0, Culture=neutral,
PublicKeyToken=31BF3856AD364E35"/>
          <add tagPrefix="asp" namespace="System.Web.UI.WebControls"
assembly="System.Web.Extensions, Version=3.5.0.0, Culture=neutral,
PublicKeyToken=31BF3856AD364E35"/>
        </controls>
```

6

LISTING 9.1   Continued

```
    </pages>

    <httpHandlers>
      <remove verb="*" path="*.asmx"/>
      <add verb="*" path="*.asmx" validate="false"
type="System.Web.Script.Services.ScriptHandlerFactory,
System.Web.Extensions, Version=3.5.0.0, Culture=neutral,
PublicKeyToken=31BF3856AD364E35"/>
      <add verb="*" path="*_AppService.axd" validate="false"
type="System.Web.Script.Services.ScriptHandlerFactory,
System.Web.Extensions, Version=3.5.0.0, Culture=neutral,
PublicKeyToken=31BF3856AD364E35"/>
      <add verb="GET,HEAD" path="ScriptResource.axd"
type="System.Web.Handlers.ScriptResourceHandler, System.Web.Extensions,
Version=3.5.0.0, Culture=neutral, PublicKeyToken=31BF3856AD364E35"
validate="false"/>
    </httpHandlers>
    <httpModules>
      <add name="ScriptModule" type="System.Web.Handlers.ScriptModule,
System.Web.Extensions, Version=3.5.0.0, Culture=neutral,
PublicKeyToken=31BF3856AD364E35"/>
    </httpModules>

  </system.web>

  <system.codedom>
    <compilers>
      <compiler language="c#;cs;csharp" extension=".cs" warningLevel="4"
                type="Microsoft.CSharp.CSharpCodeProvider, System,
Version=2.0.0.0, Culture=neutral, PublicKeyToken=b77a5c561934e089">
        <providerOption name="CompilerVersion" value="v3.5"/>
        <providerOption name="WarnAsError" value="false"/>
      </compiler>
      <compiler language="vb;vbs;visualbasic;vbscript" extension=".vb"
➥warningLevel="4"

                type="Microsoft.VisualBasic.VBCodeProvider, System,
➥Version=2.0.0.0,
 Culture=neutral, PublicKeyToken=b77a5c561934e089">
        <providerOption name="CompilerVersion" value="v3.5"/>
        <providerOption name="OptionInfer" value="true"/>
        <providerOption name="WarnAsError" value="false"/>
      </compiler>
    </compilers>
```

```
    </system.codedom>

    <!--
        The system.webServer section is required for running ASP.NET AJAX
  under Internet Information Services 7.0.  It is not necessary for previous
  version of IIS.
    -->
    <system.webServer>
      <validation validateIntegratedModeConfiguration="false"/>
      <modules>
        <remove name="ScriptModule" />
        <add name="ScriptModule" preCondition="managedHandler"
  type="System.Web.Handlers.ScriptModule, System.Web.Extensions, Version=3.5.0.0,
  Culture=neutral, PublicKeyToken=31BF3856AD364E35"/>
      </modules>
      <handlers>
        <remove name="WebServiceHandlerFactory-Integrated"/>
        <remove name="ScriptHandlerFactory" />
        <remove name="ScriptHandlerFactoryAppServices" />
        <remove name="ScriptResource" />
        <add name="ScriptHandlerFactory" verb="*" path="*.asmx"
  preCondition="integratedMode"
              type="System.Web.Script.Services.ScriptHandlerFactory,
  System.Web.Extensions, Version=3.5.0.0, Culture=neutral,
  PublicKeyToken=31BF3856AD364E35"/>
        <add name="ScriptHandlerFactoryAppServices" verb="*"
  path="*_AppService.axd"
   preCondition="integratedMode"
  type="System.Web.Script.Services.ScriptHandlerFactory, System.Web.Extensions,
  Version=3.5.0.0, Culture=neutral, PublicKeyToken=31BF3856AD364E35"/>
        <add name="ScriptResource" preCondition="integratedMode" verb="GET,HEAD"
  path="ScriptResource.axd" type="System.Web.Handlers.ScriptResourceHandler,
  System.Web.Extensions, Version=3.5.0.0, Culture=neutral,
  PublicKeyToken=31BF3856AD364E35" />
      </handlers>
    </system.webServer>

    <runtime>
      <assemblyBinding xmlns="urn:schemas-microsoft-com:asm.v1">
        <dependentAssembly>
          <assemblyIdentity name="System.Web.Extensions"
  publicKeyToken="31bf3856ad364e35"/>
          <bindingRedirect oldVersion="1.0.0.0-1.1.0.0" newVersion="3.5.0.0"/>
        </dependentAssembly>
        <dependentAssembly>
```

LISTING 9.1   Continued

```
        <assemblyIdentity name="System.Web.Extensions.Design"
publicKeyToken="31bf3856ad364e35"/>
        <bindingRedirect oldVersion="1.0.0.0-1.1.0.0" newVersion="3.5.0.0"/>
      </dependentAssembly>
    </assemblyBinding>
  </runtime>
</configuration>
```

Working from the top of the file to the bottom, notice that there are only six high-level sections of the ASP.NET Web.Config file (listed by tag name): configSections, assemblies, pages, httpHandlers, httpModules, and runtime. To enable ASP.NET AJAX in SharePoint, you need to find each of these tags in the SharePoint/WSS Web.Config file and add the settings (or child elements) that are listed under each section in the ASP.NET Web.Config file. For example, if you are searching through the SharePoint/WSS Web.Config file for the <configSections> tag, after you find it, you should paste the following code example in Listing 9.2 into this section.

LISTING 9.2   configSettings Section

```
      <sectionGroup name="system.web.extensions"
type="System.Web.Configuration.SystemWebExtensionsSectionGroup,
System.Web.Extensions, Version=3.5.0.0, Culture=neutral,
PublicKeyToken=31BF3856AD364E35">
      <sectionGroup name="scripting"
 type="System.Web.Configuration.ScriptingSectionGroup,
System.Web.Extensions, Version=3.5.0.0, Culture=neutral,
 PublicKeyToken=31BF3856AD364E35">
      <section name="scriptResourceHandler"
type="System.Web.Configuration.ScriptingScriptResourceHandlerSection,
System.Web.Extensions, Version=3.5.0.0, Culture=neutral,
PublicKeyToken=31BF3856AD364E35" requirePermission="false"
allowDefinition="MachineToApplication"/>
      <sectionGroup name="webServices"
type="System.Web.Configuration.ScriptingWebServicesSectionGroup,
System.Web.Extensions, Version=3.5.0.0, Culture=neutral,
 PublicKeyToken=31BF3856AD364E35">
      <section name="jsonSerialization"
 type="System.Web.Configuration.ScriptingJsonSerializationSection,
System.Web.Extensions, Version=3.5.0.0, Culture=neutral,
PublicKeyToken=31BF3856AD364E35"
 requirePermission="false" allowDefinition="Everywhere" />
      <section name="profileService"
 type="System.Web.Configuration.ScriptingProfileServiceSection,
System.Web.Extensions, Version=3.5.0.0, Culture=neutral,
```

```
PublicKeyToken=31BF3856AD364E35" requirePermission="false"
allowDefinition="MachineToApplication" />
        <section name="authenticationService"
type="System.Web.Configuration.ScriptingAuthenticationServiceSection,
System.Web.Extensions, Version=3.5.0.0, Culture=neutral,
PublicKeyToken=31BF3856AD364E35" requirePermission="false"
allowDefinition="MachineToApplication" />
        <section name="roleService"
 type="System.Web.Configuration.ScriptingRoleServiceSection,
System.Web.Extensions, Version=3.5.0.0, Culture=neutral,
PublicKeyToken=31BF3856AD364E35" requirePermission="false"
allowDefinition="MachineToApplication" />
      </sectionGroup>
      </sectionGroup>
    </sectionGroup>
```

You should follow this pattern for each setting in the ASP.NET Web.Config file. After you get all of your settings moved into the SharePoint/WSS Web.Config file, you should save the file and then request a page in your SharePoint instance to ensure that your Web.Config file is okay and the SharePoint site loads.

> **NOTE**
>
> It is a common occurrence to have typos in your Web.Config file when you are making changes. You should always first save a backup, make the change, and then test your site to see if there are any errors. Web.Config errors aren't the most fun to debug, so please take note.

If your site loads, and assuming that you have pasted all the sections in the right place, you are ready to begin developing ASP.NET AJAX-enabled web parts for your SharePoint/WSS sites.

Developing an AJAX-Based SharePoint Web Part

Obviously, this book is not a SharePoint development book, so the web part that will be used as an example will be simple, and the deployment of the web part will be addressed at a high level. For more information about developing SharePoint and WSS web parts, you should read a book such as *SharePoint 2007 Development Unleashed*, which covers this topic in more depth.

Developing ASP.NET AJAX-enabled SharePoint/WSS web parts is fairly simple given the skills that you have acquired earlier in this book. Basically, you need to dynamically add a

ScriptManager control and then any of the ASP.NET AJAX controls that you would like to utilize to your web part, and render it to the client. Listing 9.3 illustrates the web part that will be discussed in this chapter. Note that the project that is used for the web part is a Class Library project.

LISTING 9.3   EmployeeSales Web Part

```
using System;
using System.Collections.Generic;
using System.Linq;
using System.Text;
using Microsoft.SharePoint;
using System.Web.UI;
using System.Web.UI.WebControls;
using System.Web.UI.WebControls.WebParts;

namespace AJAX.WebParts
{
    public class EmployeeSales : WebPart
    {
        private Label lblData;

        protected override void CreateChildControls()
        {
            base.CreateChildControls();

            //fix for UpdatePanel
            EnsurePanelFix();

            //initialize controls
            Button btnGetData = new Button();
            ScriptManager scriptManager = new ScriptManager();
            UpdatePanel updPanel = new UpdatePanel();
            lblData = new Label();

            //configure controls
            lblData.ID = "lblData";
            btnGetData.ID = "btnGetData";
            btnGetData.Text = "Get Data...";
            scriptManager.ID = "scriptManager";
            updPanel.ID = "updPanel";
            updPanel.UpdateMode = UpdatePanelUpdateMode.Conditional;
            updPanel.ChildrenAsTriggers = true;

            //create the click event handler
            btnGetData.Click += new EventHandler(btnGetData_Click);
```

```
        //add button and label to UpdatePanel container
        updPanel.ContentTemplateContainer.Controls.Add(btnGetData);
        updPanel.ContentTemplateContainer.Controls.Add(lblData);

        //add the script manager and updatePanel to the web part
        this.Controls.Add(scriptManager);
        this.Controls.Add(updPanel);

    }


void btnGetData_Click(object sender, EventArgs e)
{
    SPSite site;
    SPWeb web;
    //initialize site and web
    site = new SPSite("http://moss/MyTeamSite");
    web = site.AllWebs[2];

    try
    {
        SPList employeeSales = web.Lists["Monthly Sales"];

        StringBuilder sb = new StringBuilder();
        sb.Append("<br/><br/>");
        foreach (SPListItem i in employeeSales.Items)
        {
            sb.Append(i.Title);
            sb.Append(" ");
            sb.Append(i["Total Sales"].ToString());
            sb.Append("<br/>");
        }
        lblData.Text = sb.ToString();
    }
    catch (Exception ex)
    {
        lblData.Text = ex.Message;
    }
    finally
    {
        //cleanup spWeb and spSite objects
        web.Dispose();
        site.Dispose();

    }
}
```

LISTING 9.3   Continued

```
        private void EnsurePanelFix()
        {
            if (this.Page.Form != null)
            {
                String fixupScript = @"
                    _spBodyOnLoadFunctionNames.push(""_initFormActionAjax"");
                    function _initFormActionAjax()
                    {
                      if (_spEscapedFormAction == document.forms[0].action)
                      {
                        document.forms[0]._initialAction =
                        document.forms[0].action;
                      }
                    }
                    var RestoreToOriginalFormActionCore =
                      RestoreToOriginalFormAction;
                    RestoreToOriginalFormAction = function()
                    {
                      if (_spOriginalFormAction != null)
                      {
                        RestoreToOriginalFormActionCore();
                        document.forms[0]._initialAction =
                        document.forms[0].action;
                      }
                    }";
                ScriptManager.RegisterStartupScript(this,
                  typeof(EmployeeSales), "UpdatePanelFixup",
                  fixupScript, true);
            }
        }


    }
}
```

The functionality of the web part is very simple: Get data from a SharePoint list and display it on the page. Before you learn how to do this, it is important to understand what data is available to be displayed. Figure 9.1 shows the schema of the Monthly Sales SharePoint list, and Figure 9.2 illustrates the list with sample data.

The functionality of the web part is simple in that all the controls are simply placed into an ASP.NET UpdatePanel control so that the postback will be suppressed when the user clicks on the command button. Figure 9.3 illustrates the web part as it is rendered inside a SharePoint Team Site.

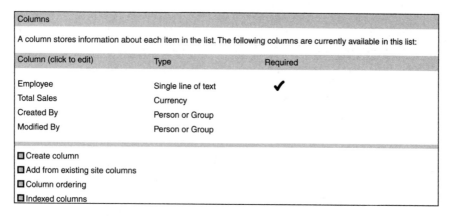

FIGURE 9.1   Monthly Sales list schema.

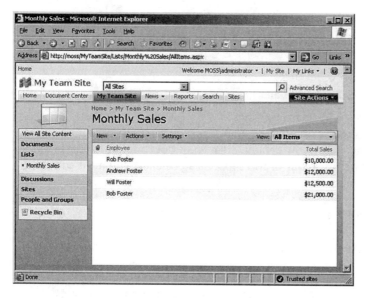

FIGURE 9.2   Monthly Sales sample data.

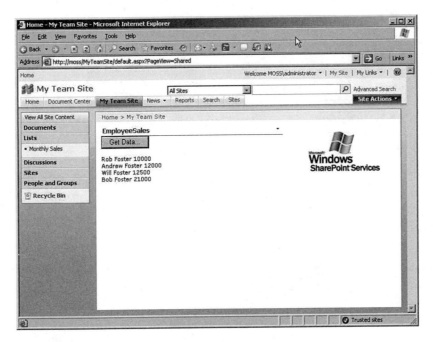

FIGURE 9.3   Web part rendered in a Team Site.

There is one simple addition to the web part that you must add to your code if you are
going to use the UpdatePanel control. By default, SharePoint does a lot of management
postbacks. Because the UpdatePanel control will suppress a postback, you must add the
following code to your web part and call it from the EnableChildControls event.

```
private void EnsurePanelFix()
{
    if (this.Page.Form != null)
    {
        String fixupScript = @"
            _spBodyOnLoadFunctionNames.push(""_initFormActionAjax"");
            function _initFormActionAjax()
            {
              if (_spEscapedFormAction == document.forms[0].action)
              {
                document.forms[0]._initialAction =
                document.forms[0].action;
              }
            }
            var RestoreToOriginalFormActionCore =
              RestoreToOriginalFormAction;
            RestoreToOriginalFormAction = function()
            {
```

```
        if (_spOriginalFormAction != null)
        {
          RestoreToOriginalFormActionCore();
          document.forms[0]._initialAction =
          document.forms[0].action;
        }
      }";
    ScriptManager.RegisterStartupScript(this,
      typeof(EmployeeSales), "UpdatePanelFixup",
      fixupScript, true);
  }
}
```

The `EnsurePanelFix` method essentially will allow SharePoint to recognize the UpdatePanel and not try to do anything "SharePoint-specific" when the control tries to postback.

Summary

With the addition of ASP.NET AJAX to your SharePoint development tool belt, you will now be able to create very robust and interactive ASP.NET AJAX-enabled web parts that can help enable a positive user experience for your users who use the SharePoint platform. In this chapter, you learned how to configure SharePoint/WSS to recognize ASP.NET AJAX and how to build a simple ASP.NET AJAX-enabled web part.

CHAPTER 10

Creating ASP.NET AJAX-Enabled Vista Sidebar Gadgets

Vista Sidebar Gadgets are simple applications that give users immediate access to personally relevant information and simple tasks. Gadgets are hosted in the Windows Vista Sidebar, which is located on the right side of your desktop (assuming that you are running Windows Vista as your operating system). In short, Gadgets typically perform a single task very easily and efficiently and can be customized to give you information that you want.

Vista Sidebar Gadgets

Typical examples of Gadgets include a stock ticker, clock, weather, news feeds, and so on. The stock ticker enables you to add your own stocks that you would like to monitor and gives you the ability to customize the Gadget to display only the stocks that you want to see. The same is true for the Weather Gadget. You simply add the Weather Gadget to your sidebar and type in your ZIP code, and you will get weather updates delivered directly to your desktop. Figure 10.1 illustrates the Windows Vista Sidebar with some sample Gadgets added.

As you can see in Figure 10.1, several Gadgets are running in the Vista Sidebar. The first two are examples of the Presto Clock (downloaded from the online Gadget library), which is used to show the times in two different time zones. This also highlights another important feature of Gadgets: You can have multiple instances of the same Gadget running on your Sidebar.

You can easily add new Gadgets to the Vista Sidebar by right-clicking the Sidebar and selecting the Add Gadget option. This displays the Add Gadget dialog window, which shows a list of Gadgets that you currently have installed on your computer. If you are looking for something more specific, you can also search the online Gadget gallery by clicking the Get More Gadgets Online link. Figure 10.2 shows the Add Gadget dialog window.

FIGURE 10.1   Windows Vista Gadget Sidebar.

FIGURE 10.2   Add Gadget dialog window.

With all these cool and usable Gadgets available, why would you want to go to the trouble of writing your own Gadget? As discussed in the previous paragraphs, Gadgets are used to give users information that is relevant to them. This might include data that exists on your corporate intranet. If this is the case, then you most likely won't be able to go to the Internet and download a Gadget that will meet the needs of your users, and you will need to custom-build something. Conversely, if you *can* go to the Internet and download a

Gadget that publicly exposes your corporate data, then maybe you should stop reading now and go secure your network.

Building Gadgets is very easy to do. In the next section, you learn how to build an ASP.NET AJAX-enabled Gadget.

Creating the Gadget

Creating an ASP.NET AJAX-enabled Gadget is similar to creating an ASP.NET AJAX-enabled web page. In the following examples, you learn how to create a Gadget that displays a random number which is generated and returned by a web service. This is a simple example so that you can focus on the fundamentals of the Gadget code without having to interpret the inner workings of a complex example. First, you need to create the web service that will be called by the Gadget.

Create the Web Service

Creating the web service for this example is a simple process. You need to create a new ASP.NET web site, as illustrated in Figure 10.3.

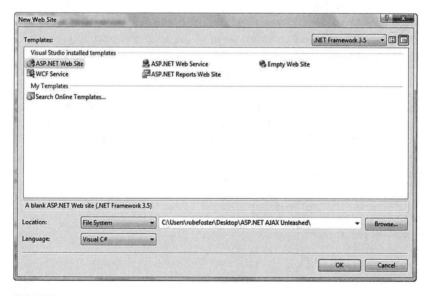

FIGURE 10.3   Create a new ASP.NET web site.

After you have a web site, you need to add a new AJAX-enabled web service to your project. In this example, it is named Service.svc. Figure 10.4 illustrates creating the AJAX-enabled WCF Service.

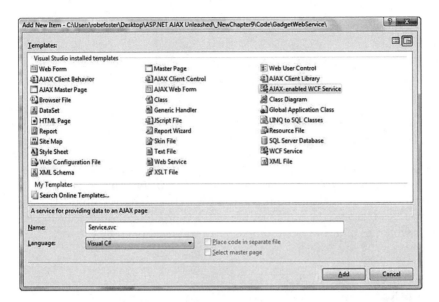

FIGURE 10.4   Create a new AJAX-enabled WCF Service.

> **NOTE**
>
> By creating the AJAX-enabled WCF Service, you will be able to easily generate a JavaScript proxy so that your service can be called by client-side code. You can use a regular WCF Service, but you will have to manually write all the JavaScript plumbing code. Using an AJAX-enabled WCF Service will help you save a lot of time and effort.

After you have added a new AJAX-enabled WCF Service to your web site, you can begin to create the logic behind your service. In this example, it's a simple function that will return a random number between 1 and 10. Listing 10.1 illustrates the AJAX-enabled WCF Service.

LISTING 10.1   Random Number Generator AJAX-Enabled WCF Service

```
using System;
using System.Linq;
using System.Runtime.Serialization;
using System.ServiceModel;
using System.ServiceModel.Activation;
using System.ServiceModel.Web;

[ServiceContract(Namespace = "")]
[AspNetCompatibilityRequirements(
RequirementsMode = AspNetCompatibilityRequirementsMode.Allowed)]
public class Service
{
```

```
/// <summary>
/// Get a random number between 1 and 10
/// </summary>
/// <returns>Random number as int</returns>
[OperationContract]
public int GetRandomNumber()
{
    Random r = new Random();
    return r.Next(0, 10);
}
}
```

After you have your service created, you are ready to create the JavaScript proxy that will be inserted into the code for your new Gadget.

Generate the JavaScript Proxy

When you are using an AJAX-enabled WCF Service, generating a JavaScript proxy is very easy. From Visual Studio, set the Service.svc service as the startup page, and then click run. This will start up the Visual Studio debugger and open Internet Explorer, which displays a common web service information page, as illustrated in Figure 10.5.

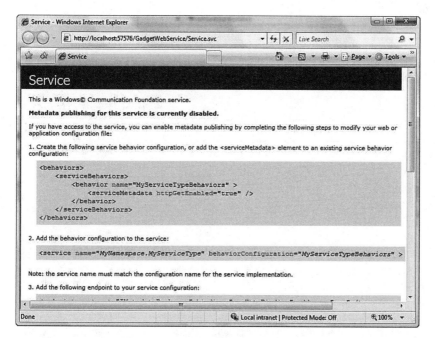

FIGURE 10.5 Viewing the WCF Service in Internet Explorer.

In this setup, Visual Studio has configured the ASP.NET Development Server to host the site on port 57576. This likely will be different when you run it locally on your machine, so be aware that the URL could look a bit different when you are testing this yourself.

Notice the URL that is displayed: http://localhost:57576/GadgetWebService/Service.svc. You can generate a JavaScript proxy for this web service by adding a /js to the end of your URL so that the URL is now as follows: http://localhost:57576/GadgetWebService/Service.svc/js.

When you add the /js suffix to the end of your URL, you will be prompted with a dialog window to save the file, as shown in Figure 10.6.

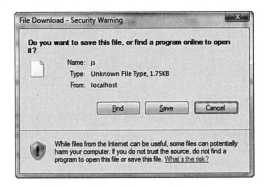

FIGURE 10.6   Save the JavaScript Proxy.

Click the Save button to save the JavaScript Proxy and name it Proxy.js (or some unique name that you can remember). When you save the proxy and open it in Notepad or Visual Studio, it should resemble what is shown in Listing 10.2.

LISTING 10.2   JavaScript Proxy

```
var Service=function() {
Service.initializeBase(this);
this._timeout = 0;
this._userContext = null;
this._succeeded = null;
this._failed = null;
}
Service.prototype={
_get_path:function() {
 var p = this.get_path();
 if (p) return p;
 else return Service._staticInstance.get_path();},
GetRandomNumber:function(succeededCallback, failedCallback, userContext)
 {
```

```
return this._invoke(this._get_path(),
 'GetRandomNumber',false,{},succeededCallback,
failedCallback,userContext); }}
Service.registerClass('Service',Sys.Net.WebServiceProxy);
Service._staticInstance = new Service();
Service.set_path = function(value) {
Service._staticInstance.set_path(value); }
Service.get_path = function() {
return Service._staticInstance.get_path(); }
Service.set_timeout = function(value) {
Service._staticInstance.set_timeout(value); }
Service.get_timeout = function() {
return Service._staticInstance.get_timeout(); }
Service.set_defaultUserContext = function(value) {
Service._staticInstance.set_defaultUserContext(value); }
Service.get_defaultUserContext = function() { return
Service._staticInstance.get_defaultUserContext(); }
Service.set_defaultSucceededCallback = function(value) {
Service._staticInstance.set_defaultSucceededCallback(value); }
Service.get_defaultSucceededCallback = function() {
return Service._staticInstance.get_defaultSucceededCallback(); }
Service.set_defaultFailedCallback = function(value) {
Service._staticInstance.set_defaultFailedCallback(value); }
Service.get_defaultFailedCallback = function() {
return Service._staticInstance.get_defaultFailedCallback(); }
Service.set_path("/GadgetWebService/Service.svc");
Service.GetRandomNumber= function(onSuccess,onFailed,userContext)
 {Service._staticInstance.GetRandomNumber(
onSuccess,onFailed,userContext);
}
```

The generated proxy can *almost* be used straight out of the box as it is generated. Notice that there is one line in the code that is bold. In this example (as with most Gadgets), it is likely that the web service will exist in another location from where the Gadget is running. Because this is the case, you need to modify the code to reflect the location of the service. In this example, it is pointed at the ASP.NET Development Server, where the service is exposed on port 57576. So, the Service.set_path statement will need to be modified as listed in the following code line. Note that you will need to modify the URL to reflect the location that your service is running.

```
Service.set_path("http://localhost:57576/GadgetWebService/Service.svc");
```

After you make this modification, save the Proxy.js file again and you are ready to create the code behind your Gadget.

Create the Vista Gadget

There are several things that you need to do to create a Gadget. First, you need to understand how Gadgets are deployed to a Vista machine. Custom Gadgets are deployed to the C:\Users*<yourUserName>*\AppData\Local\Microsoft\Windows Sidebar\Gadgets\ directory, where *<yourUserName>* is your logon ID. You need to navigate to this directory and create a new subdirectory called "GetRandomNumber.gadget". This is where you need to place a few files to support the Gadget. The first two files are your web service proxy JavaScript file and the Microsoft ASP.NET AJAX client-side library, which can be downloaded from the following location: http://ajax.asp.net/downloads/library/default.aspx?tabid=47&subtabid=471.

When you load this URL, you will be prompted to sign the EULA for the ASP.NET AJAX library and then presented with the option to download a ZIP file that contains the library. You will find a file named MicrosoftAJAX.en-US.js in this ZIP file, which you will need to copy to the GetRandomNumber.gadget directory so that your Gadget will be able to reference this library.

Up to this point, you should have two files in your GetRandomNumber.gadget directory: proxy.js and MicrosoftAjax.en-US.js. Now you are ready to create the code that will define the functionality behind your Gadget.

First, you need to create a file called Gadget.xml, which will describe your Gadget. Listing 10.3 illustrates the Gadget.xml file for the GetRandomNumber Gadget.

LISTING 10.3   Gadget.xml

```
<?xml version="1.0" encoding="utf-8" ?>
<gadget>
  <name>Get Random Number</name>
  <version>1.0</version>
  <hosts>
    <host name="sidebar">
      <base type="HTML" apiVersion="1.0.0" src="GetRandomNumber.html" />
      <permissions>full</permissions>
      <platform minPlatformVersion="0.3" />
    </host>
  </hosts>
</gadget>
```

The important elements that you should notice in the Gadget.xml file are the <name> and <base> elements. The <name> element allows you to create a user-friendly name for your Gadget. This is the property that will get displayed to users when they add your Gadget to the Windows Vista Sidebar, so you should make this property as descriptive as reasonably possible.

The <base> element contains an attribute called src, which defines *where* the UI for your Gadget is located. In this example, it is contained within a file named GetRandomNumber.html, which is described in Listing 10.4.

LISTING 10.4   GetRandomNumber.html

```html
<html>
<head>
    <title>Random Numbers</title>
    <script type="text/javascript" src="MicrosoftAjax.en-US.js"></script>
    <script type="text/javascript" src="proxy.js"></script>
</head>
<body style="width:100%;height:150px">
<input id="btn" type="button" value="Get Num" onclick="btn_click(); return false;" />
<br />
Random Number: <span id="spnNumber"></span>
</body>
<script type="text/javascript">
    function btn_click() {
        Service.GetRandomNumber(function (result) {
            $get('spnNumber').innerHTML = result;
        });
    }
</script>
</html>
```

Notice the script references to the Microsoft ASP.NET AJAX client library and the web service proxy. In this example, these references are required because the majority of your client-side JavaScript code is contained in these files. Following the code, you will notice that a button and a span have been defined to give the user some interaction with the Gadget itself. When the user clicks the button, the web service will be called and a random number between 1 and 10 will be placed inside the span.

This brings you to the button's click event. This event calls the Service.GetRandomNumber function, which is defined in the Proxy.js file, and the results are inserted into the span's innerHTML property.

As you can see from these examples, creating Gadgets is quite a simple process. In the next section, you learn how to test your new Gadget.

Test the Gadget

Testing the Gadget is a simple process. You need to right-click your Sidebar and then select the Add Gadgets option. This displays the Add Gadgets dialog window, which is illustrated in Figure 10.7.

FIGURE 10.7   Add Gadget Dialog Window with new Gadget.

You can drag and drop the Get Random Number Gadget into your Vista Sidebar, and it will display in the Sidebar. When you click on the Get Num button, the random number web service will be called and a random number between 1 and 10 will be generated and displayed in the Gadget, as shown in Figure 10.8.

FIGURE 10.8   Get Random Number Gadget in Sidebar.

Summary

In this chapter, you have learned how to leverage your ASP.NET AJAX skills to build Windows Vista Gadgets for the Vista Sidebar. Combining the skills of ASP.NET AJAX and Windows Vista Gadgets can help you provide more dynamic and robust user experiences to your end users.

PART III

Appendices

IN THIS PART

Microsoft Expression Web

Microsoft Expression Web is a web design tool that you can use for designing rich user interfaces for your web applications. For application developers who use Visual Studio for all development, Expression Web might be perceived as "just another tool" that you can get the same results with by using Visual Studio. For larger teams, however, you might have dedicated web designers who are responsible solely for user interface design. Expression Web gives them the familiar interface of a web design tool without having to learn the complexity of Visual Studio. In this chapter, you learn about Microsoft Expression Web and its features as a web design tool.

An Introduction to the Expression Web Interface

When you first open Expression Web, you will notice that it has an interface similar to what you would see in Visual Studio: there are dockable panes on each side of the screen, and your work surface is in the middle. This enables you to very easily customize the user interface. Figure A.1 illustrates the Expression Web user interface.

Creating Web Pages and Web Sites

Many templates are available to you as a web designer that can be used to create a variety of web sites and web pages. These templates can be used as a starting point to help set up your web site layout.

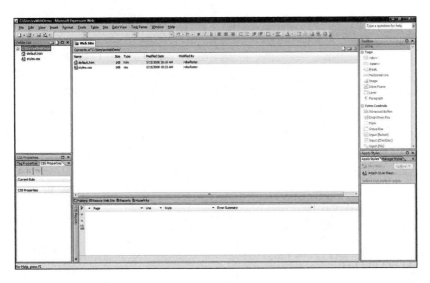

FIGURE A.1   Expression Web user interface

Create a New Web Page

When you go to the File -> New menu, you have the option to create a new page or web site. The option to create a new page allows you to create and edit single web pages, without associating them with or creating a new web site. Figure A.2 shows the options that can be used to create a new web page.

The most common options are listed on the General tab of the New Page dialog and include the following:

- ▶ **HTML**—Creates a basic HTML page.
- ▶ **ASPX**—Creates an ASPX page.
- ▶ **CSS**—Creates a cascading style sheet.
- ▶ **Master Page**—Creates an ASP.NET master page that will be associated with an ASPX page.
- ▶ **Dynamic Web Template**—Dynamic Web Templates (DWTs) are similar to ASP.NET Master Pages, but are associated with an Expression Web Site. It is most similar to a FrontPage Theme and allows you to apply a custom theme to your web site.
- ▶ **JavaScript**—Creates a new JavaScript file.
- ▶ **XML**—Creates a new XML file.
- ▶ **Text File**—Creates a new text file.
- ▶ **Create from Dynamic Web Template**—Creates a page that is associated with a specified Dynamic Web Template (or Theme).
- ▶ **Create from Master Page**—Creates a page that is associated with a specified ASP.NET master page.

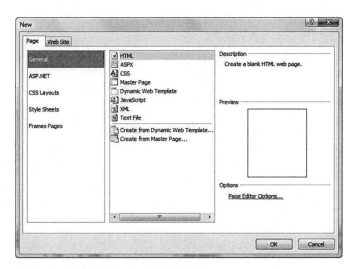

FIGURE A.2   Create a new web page.

You will notice that when creating pages (such as ASPX), you only have access to the ASPX UI code and design layout. When you create a new ASPX file, you will not get any of the code behind (such as .cs, .vb) or resource files (.resx) that you typically have access to in Visual Studio. Expression Web is meant to allow you to focus on the pages user interface elements, and not distract you with the complexities of the managed code.

Create a New Web Site

The New Web Site option enables you to use Expression Web to create a new web site. It is important to note that some pages (such as ASPX) will require a web server so that they can be processed and rendered to the browser. Fortunately, you will not need to install Internet Information Services (IIS) on your desktop. Like Visual Studio, Expression Web comes with the ASP.NET Development Server so that you can view the pages that require a web server to process and render. Figure A.3 illustrates the Create New Web Site dialog.

Two categories of web sites can be used to create a new web site:

▶ **General**—Creates a simple web site

▶ **Templates**—Creates a web site based on a DWT

Creating web sites that can be used as the foundations for your overall solution is one feature because you as the web designer have full control of how the pages are laid out, where they are located physically in the web site (what directories), as well as how they link and are related to one another (either by using Master Pages or DWTs). After the directory structure is created (or evolved) and the files are created that define the look and feel of your web site, it can be handed off to a development team using Visual Studio, who can plug in the managed code and deploy the web site.

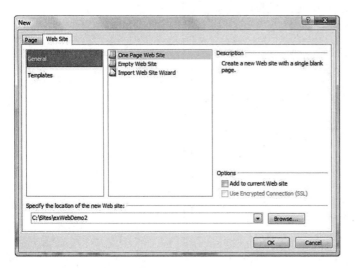

FIGURE A.3   Create a new web site.

Customizable Interface

Expression Web has a highly customizable interface consisting of (by default) six task panes that will increase your productivity:

▶ Folder List

▶ Tag Properties

▶ CSS Properties

▶ Toolbox

▶ Apply Styles

▶ Manage Styles

Folder List

The Folder list task pane lists the files and folders that are contained in your web site. This is similar to the Solution Explorer in Visual Studio. Figure A.4 illustrates the Folder List pane of a web site called exWebDemo.

The Folder List is used as a web site file manager and enables you to create, rename, and delete files that are in your web. You can drag files from your folder list to the design pane of Expression Web to create links to pages. When you do this, Expression Web knows where all links to the file exist so that if the filename or file location ever change, it will automatically update this link in all pages that reference the file.

FIGURE A.4   Folder List task pane

Tag Properties

The Tag Properties task pane is used to quickly view and set the available properties for a selected HTML or ASP.NET tag. This dialog is similar to the Properties window in Visual Studio. Listing A.1 shows the code from an ASP.NET page called default.aspx.

LISTING A.1   Default.aspx

```
<!DOCTYPE html PUBLIC "-//W3C//DTD XHTML 1.0 Transitional//EN"
 "http://www.w3.org/TR/xhtml1/DTD/xhtml1-transitional.dtd">
<%@ Page Language="C#" %>
<html dir="ltr" xmlns="http://www.w3.org/1999/xhtml">

<head runat="server">
<meta http-equiv="Content-Type" content="text/html; charset=utf-8" />
<title>Home</title>
</head>

<body>

<form id="form1" runat="server">
    <asp:Button runat="server" ID="cmdClickMe" Text="Click Me ">
    </asp:Button>
</form>

</body>
</html>
```

You can see in the code example that the page contains one button called cmdClickMe. When this button is selected, the Tag Properties task pane will show the properties of the ASP.NET Button control, as illustrated in Figure A.5.

There are a few things to note about Figure A.5. First, just like the Visual Studio Properties window, you can categorize and sort the Properties window. Notice that the properties are selected to be displayed in alphabetical order, and the properties that have been set are listed at the top in bold typeface. Also, if you look between the categorize buttons and the properties, the type of control is listed. In this example, it is listed as

FIGURE A.5   Tag Properties task pane

`<asp:Button#cmdClickMe>`, which indicates that you are looking at the properties for an ASP.NET Button control named `cmdClickMe`.

CSS Properties

The CSS Properties task pane is used to view and set properties of items in a cascading style sheet (CSS). The following CSS code is from a file called styles.css.

```
.boldLabel {
    font-family: "Times New Roman", Times, serif;
    font-size: 12pt;
    font-weight: bold;
    font-variant: normal;
}
```

When you select this item in your CSS files (place the cursor anywhere in the code), its properties are displayed in the CSS Properties task pane as displayed in Figure A.6.

Toolbox

The Toolbox task pane enables you to drag and drop controls directly onto your web page. It contains two categories of items: HTML and ASP.NET. The HTML category contains all HTML controls, such as standard tags like SPAN and DIV, and form controls, such as a submit button and inputs (button, textbox, and so forth).

The ASP.NET category contains standard ASP.NET Controls and is only available when you are editing an ASP.NET web page. Figure A.7 shows the Toolbox task pane.

FIGURE A.6   CSS Properties task pane

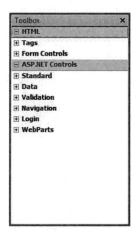

FIGURE A.7   Toolbox task pane

Apply Styles

The Apply Styles task pane can be used to create new styles in a new or existing style sheet, attach a style sheet to a web page, and associate styles with elements on a page. Figure A.8 shows the Apply Styles task pane.

FIGURE A.8   Apply Styles task pane

Manage Styles

The Manage Styles task pane gives you the ability to create new styles in the associated style sheet as well as to preview styles that are defined by the style sheet. Figure A.9 shows the Manage Styles task pane, which is being used to display a preview of the .boldLabel style that is defined in the styles.css style sheet.

Similar to Visual Studio, these task panes can be dragged and docked in any of the four dockable regions inside Expression Web. This enables you to easily customize the interface and place the task panes where you want them so that you can be most productive.

Creating Standards-Based Web Sites

Expression Web allows you to easily create standards-based web sites using HTML, XML, XSL, and CSS. You can take many different approaches to create the standard look and feel of a web site. In this section, you learn how to quickly build sites using Dynamic Web Templates (DWTs), look at different coding views, and learn how Expression Web supports code snippits.

Quickly Build Standards-Based Sites

You can quickly build a standards-based web site by creating a web site based on a dynamic web template. This can be done easily by creating a new web site based on a template, as shown in the Create New Web site dialog in Figure A.10.

FIGURE A.9   Manage Styles task pane

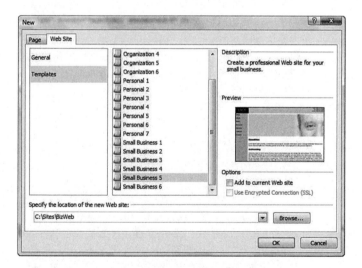

FIGURE A.10   Create New DWT-based Web site

In Figure A.10, a new web site called BizWeb is being created that is based on the Small Business 5 template. When you click the OK button, a new DWT-based web site will be created.

The template creates a few files and directories that will help you set up and configure your site. These directories and files are shown in Figure A.11.

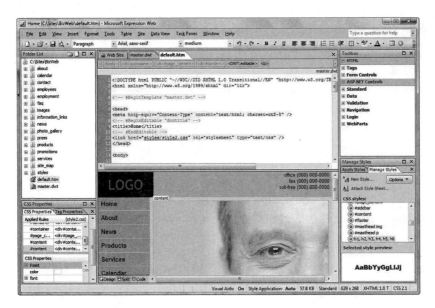

FIGURE A.11   Small Business 5 site in Expression Web

As you can see in Figure A.11, there are a number of files and directories now contained in the Folder List task pane. One of those files is named master.dwt. This is the DWT file that is used as the base template for the site. The DWT gives the page a common layout and feel, so changes that are made to the DWT file will affect every page that uses it as a template. Figure A.12 illustrates the Small Business 5 site as it is rendered out of the box in Internet Explorer.

Looking at Figure A.11, you will notice that you can switch between different code views in Expression Web, similar to the way that you can in Visual Studio. Figure A.11 is showing the split mode between code and design, but you can easily select the Code or Design buttons to look at the code-only, or the design-only views of the web page.

Up until this point, you have learned that you can use Expression Web to create web sites that have a standard look and feel. You can also have it ensure that the HTML code generated by Expression Web complies with a specific HTML or CSS standard. If you look at the following excerpt from Listing A.1 (which is from the first line of the listing), you can see that this page will follow the XHTML 1.0 Transitional standards, which are the standards that most web designers say you should be using on web sites today.

```
<!DOCTYPE html PUBLIC "-//W3C//DTD XHTML 1.0 Transitional//EN"
 "http://www.w3.org/TR/xhtml1/DTD/xhtml1-transitional.dtd">
```

You can easily change the standard that is used for your page by clicking on the Tools -> Page Editor Options menu item inside Expression Web. Figure A.13 illustrates the authoring tab of the Page Editor Options.

FIGURE A.12   Small Business 5 site in Internet Explorer

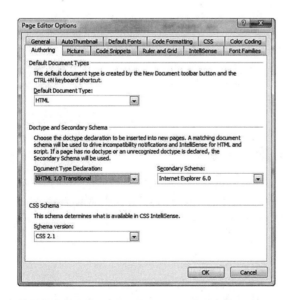

FIGURE A.13   Change the web page standard

To change the standard by which your page will implement, select from the list of Document Type Declaration (DTD) listed in the Doctype and Secondary Schema section of the Authoring Tab.

You can use the following valid DTDs for your pages:

- None
- HTML 4.01 Frameset
- HTML 4.01 Strict
- HTML 4.01 Transitional
- XHTML 1.0 Frameset
- XHTML 1.0 Strict
- XHTML 1.0 Transitional
- XHTML 1.1

From the Authoring tab, you can also change the CSS Schema that is used on your site. You can select from the following valid CSS Schemas:

- CSS 1.0
- CSS 2.0
- CSS 2.1
- CSS IE6

Note that changing the page's DTD or the site's CSS Schema will alter the IntelliSense that you will get when editing files inside of Expression Web. You will also get validation errors when you try to code something that doesn't comply with the selected standard.

Code Formatting and IntelliSense

You will find that Expression Web has a lot of the same code formatting and IntelliSense that you find in more advanced developer tools such as Visual Studio. In this section, you see how to autoformat your code as well as look at the IntelliSense features of Expression Web.

Autoformatting Code

Expression Web has a lot of settings for automatically formatting your code as it is developed. One of the problems with the previous generation tools (FrontPage) was that these tools would reformat code to meet the standards of the tool, not the user.

You can view the code formatting options by clicking on the Tools -> Page Editor Options menu item and then selecting the Code Formatting tab. Figure A.14 illustrates the Code Formatting tab.

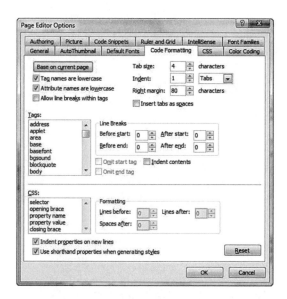

FIGURE A.14   Code Formatting options

As you can quickly see in Figure A.14, you have a lot of control over how your code gets automatically formatted in Expression Web. You can either customize the Code Formatting options to meet your needs, or you can base them on the current page that is open in the Expression Web designer window. This will help you conform to the standards of the current page that is loaded in the designer.

Along with the Code Formatting options, you also have options to optimize your code so that it presents a lighter weight footprint when rendered to the browser. You can set the code optimization options by clicking the Tools -> Optimize HTML menu item, which is shown in Figure A.15.

The categories of HTML optimization options enable you to remove HTML comments, whitespace, unused content, or generated HTML. You have a lot of flexibility when optimizing your code, but you need to be careful: Once your code has been optimized, you need to reformat your HTML by right-clicking in the code window and then clicking Reformat HTML from the popup menu.

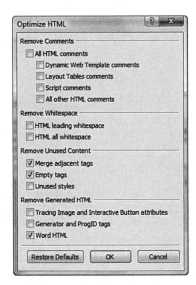

FIGURE A.15   HTML optimization options

IntelliSense

There are quite a few IntelliSense features that are available in Expression Web. IntelliSense is a context-sensitive menu that helps you to write code. If you are in the code window in Expression Web, you can either start typing a tag or press the Ctrl key and then press Enter to activate IntelliSense. Figure A.16 shows an example of the IntelliSense features of Expression Web.

You can be much more productive by using IntelliSense because you don't have to remember all the attributes of a particular tag (HTML, ASP.NET, and XML). IntelliSense also works with JavaScript, which if you do a lot of client-side scripting, this functionality is almost essential for productivity in writing JavaScript code.

XML and XSLT Tools in Expression Web

The XML and XSLT features of Expression Web alone are worth the price of the product. You can easily create views of XML data in your pages by dragging an XML file into your page and generating an XSLT style sheet for the XML. In this section, you learn about the rich XML and XSLT features of Expression Web.

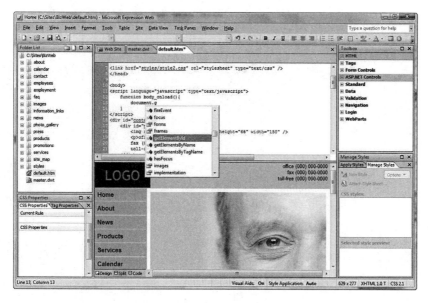

FIGURE A.16   Expression Web IntelliSense

Drag and Drop XML

The XML in Listing A.2 will be used for the examples discussed in this section.

LISTING A.2   Products.xml

```
<products>
    <product>
        <name>Shirt</name>
        <color>Blue</color>
        <price>$125.00</price>
    </product>
    <product>
        <name>Hat</name>
        <color>Red</color>
        <price>$75.00</price>
    </product>
    <product>
        <name>Pants</name>
        <color>Black</color>
        <price>$165.00</price>
    </product>
</products>
```

After you have created the products.xml file, you can begin to use it in your Expression Web projects. To begin using this file, simply drag and drop it onto the design surface, and you will see the data displayed as a grid inside the web page (see Figure A.17).

FIGURE A.17   XML rendered as a grid

What actually happens behind the scenes is that Expression Web will create a data view and associate it with some basic XSLT to the XML file that is being displayed on the page. By default, the rendering will occur at the server side, but it can easily be changed to process on the client. You can change these settings by selecting the data view (or the grid in the designer), clicking the arrow in the upper-right corner of the control, and then clicking on the Data View Properties option. This option displays a dialog box that can be used to set the processing location of the XML, as shown in Figure A.18.

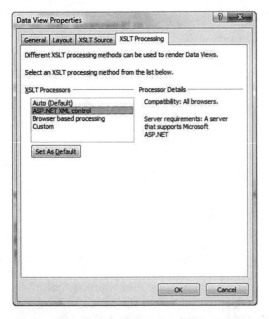

FIGURE A.18   Setting the XSLT Processing location

Creating and Updating XSL

After you have configured your Data View to render XML as described earlier in this section, you will be prompted to save the XSLT file that does the actual rendering. By default, it will render a grid, but the generated XSLT can serve as a good starting point for writing custom XSLT. Listing A.3 illustrates the XSLT that was generated to render the products.xml file.

LISTING A.3   Products.xsl

```xsl
<xsl:stylesheet version="1.0" exclude-result-prefixes="xsl ddwrt msxsl"
 xmlns:ddwrt="http://schemas.microsoft.com/WebParts/v2/DataView/runtime"
 xmlns:xsl="http://www.w3.org/1999/XSL/Transform"
xmlns:msxsl="urn:schemas-microsoft-com:xslt"
xmlns:ddwrt2="urn:frontpage:internal">
    <xsl:param name="dvt_adhocmode"></xsl:param>
    <xsl:param name="dvt_adhocfiltermode">xsl</xsl:param>
    <xsl:param name="dvt_fieldsort"></xsl:param>
    <xsl:param name="dvt_sortfield"></xsl:param>
    <xsl:param name="dvt_groupfield"></xsl:param>
    <xsl:param name="dvt_groupdisplay"></xsl:param>
    <xsl:param name="dvt_sortdir">ascending</xsl:param>
    <xsl:param name="dvt_groupdir">ascending</xsl:param>
    <xsl:param name="dvt_grouptype"></xsl:param>
    <xsl:param name="dvt_sorttype">text</xsl:param>
    <xsl:param name="dvt_groupsorttype">text</xsl:param>
    <xsl:param name="dvt_filterfield"></xsl:param>
    <xsl:param name="dvt_filterval"></xsl:param>
    <xsl:param name="dvt_filtertype"></xsl:param>
    <xsl:param name="dvt_firstrow">1</xsl:param>
    <xsl:param name="dvt_nextpagedata"></xsl:param>
    <xsl:param name="dvt_apos">'</xsl:param>
    <xsl:param name="filterParam"></xsl:param>
    <xsl:template match="/">
        <xsl:call-template name="dvt_1"/>
    </xsl:template>
    <xsl:template name="dvt_1">
        <xsl:variable name="StyleName">Table</xsl:variable>
        <xsl:variable name="Rows" select="/products/product"/>
        <xsl:variable name="RowCount" select="count($Rows)"/>
        <xsl:variable name="IsEmpty" select="$RowCount = 0"/>
        <xsl:choose>
            <xsl:when test="$IsEmpty">
                <xsl:call-template name="dvt_1.empty"/>
            </xsl:when>
            <xsl:otherwise>
                <table border="0" width="100%"
```

LISTING A.3 Continued

```
cellpadding="2" cellspacing="0">
                        <tr valign="top">
                            <th class="ms-vh" nowrap="nowrap">name</th>
                            <th class="ms-vh" nowrap="nowrap">color</th>
                            <th class="ms-vh" nowrap="nowrap">price</th>
                        </tr>
                        <xsl:call-template name="dvt_1.body">
                            <xsl:with-param name="Rows" select="$Rows"/>
                            <xsl:with-param name="FirstRow" select="1"/>
                            <xsl:with-param name="LastRow" select="$RowCount"/>
                        </xsl:call-template>
                    </table>
                </xsl:otherwise>
            </xsl:choose>
        </xsl:template>
        <xsl:template name="dvt_1.body">
            <xsl:param name="Rows"/>
            <xsl:param name="FirstRow"/>
            <xsl:param name="LastRow"/>
            <xsl:for-each select="$Rows">
                <xsl:variable name="KeepItemsTogether" select="false()"/>
                <xsl:variable name="HideGroupDetail" select="false()"/>
                <xsl:variable name="GroupStyle" select="'auto'"/>
                <xsl:if test="true()">
                    <xsl:if test="not($HideGroupDetail)" ddwrt:cf_ignore="1">
                        <tr style="display:{$GroupStyle}">
                            <td class="ms-vb">
                                <xsl:value-of select="name"/>
                            </td>
                            <td class="ms-vb">
                                <xsl:value-of select="color"/>
                            </td>
                            <td class="ms-vb">
                                <xsl:value-of select="price"/>
                            </td>
                        </tr>
                    </xsl:if>
                </xsl:if>
            </xsl:for-each>
        </xsl:template>
        <xsl:template name="dvt_1.empty">
            <xsl:variable name="ViewEmptyText">There are no
items to show in this view.</xsl:variable>
            <table border="0" width="100%">
```

```
            <tr>
                <td class="ms-vb">
                    <xsl:value-of select="$ViewEmptyText"/>
                </td>
            </tr>
        </table>
    </xsl:template>
</xsl:stylesheet>
```

You can apply sorting and filtering rules with Expression Web to sort and filter the rendered XML. This is simply a wizard that will add the appropriate clauses to the XSL document to either sort or filter the data.

Summary

In this chapter, you learned about Microsoft Expression Web and how it can be used to design fully functional user experiences. Expression Web provides you with a lot of power and flexibility to design web pages as well as quickly prototype mockups for user interfaces using a common web design tool.

Deploying the .NET Framework 3.5 as a SharePoint Feature

Features and Solutions

A best practice for deploying modifications to SharePoint (Web Parts, Web.Config modifications, event receivers, and so on) is to use a SharePoint feature. SharePoint features (or "features") are simply deployable units of functionality that can be deployed to and shared across your SharePoint farm. After being deployed, features can be activated or deactivated based on where they are scoped. For example, a feature that is scoped to the web application level must be activated at that level and it will not show up as a feature of your subsite collections or sites.

You aren't required to use features for deployments, but they simplify the process of updating your deployed components across your servers and environments. For example, you will probably not deploy components as features while you are developing them locally because you will be constantly refining them and deploying to your local environment. However, as soon as you are ready to ship your developed components to a shared environment (like a QA or production environment), you should consider deploying them as a feature. In this section, you learn how to create a feature that will modify the Web.Config file so that SharePoint will use the .NET Framework 3.5 and ASP.NET 3.5 AJAX.

As previously discussed, a feature is simply a deployable unit of code that you can deploy to your SharePoint environment. Features can be scoped to either the web, site, web application, or farm levels. The "allowed" capabilities of the feature that you create for deployment depend on how the feature is scoped. The following is a list of capabilities that can be deployed depending on a feature's scope.

Farm (SharePoint Farm)

- ▶ Control
- ▶ Control action
- ▶ Control action group
- ▶ Feature to site template association
- ▶ Custom action

Web Application (SharePoint Web Application)

- ▶ Control
- ▶ Custom action
- ▶ Document converter
- ▶ Feature to site template association
- ▶ Web.Config modifications

Site (SharePoint Site Collection)

- ▶ Content type
- ▶ Content type binding
- ▶ Control
- ▶ Custom action
- ▶ Feature to site template association
- ▶ Field
- ▶ List template
- ▶ Module
- ▶ Workflow

Web (SharePoint Site)

- ▶ Control
- ▶ Custom action
- ▶ List instance
- ▶ List template
- ▶ Module
- ▶ Receiver

Given this set of capabilities, to modify the Web.Config file (because it resides at the SharePoint web application level), you will need to create a feature that is scoped to the web application.

A SharePoint solution (or "solution") is another deployable unit that you can use to deploy multiple features to your farm. It is similar to an MSI file that is used to set up and configure multiple files when you install an application on your desktop. Solutions are very useful, specifically if you have features that need to be deployed together. In the next section, you will create a single SharePoint feature that is packaged and deployed with a solution file.

Creating the Solution

At the time this manuscript was written, there were over 200 SharePoint-related projects on the Microsoft open source CodePlex site (http://www.codeplex.com). A lot of these tools are very valuable if you are a SharePoint developer. One of them is called STSDev and is a helper application for creating Visual Studio projects that are configured for creating and deploying SharePoint features and solutions. Surprisingly, manually creating a Visual Studio project for a feature/solution isn't intuitive and this tool simplifies the process. You can download STSDev from the following link: http://www.codeplex.com/stsdev.

NOTE

Note the following development machine virtual machine configuration:

- ▶ Windows Server 2003 R2, Standard Edition
- ▶ Visual Studio 2008
- ▶ SQL Server 2005
- ▶ SharePoint 2007 Enterprise Edition
- ▶ Office 2007 Ultimate Edition

After downloading and unzipping STSDev (there is no installer), you can open STSDev to start creating your solution. Figure B.1 illustrates the STSDev tool as it is being used to create a Visual Studio project called ThreeFive that is a SharePoint solution.

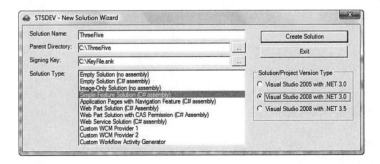

FIGURE B.1   Using the STSDev tool.

STSDev automatically creates a Visual Studio project that will be used to create the modifications to the Web.Config file. There are options to create the solution using either Visual Studio 2005 (.NET 3.0) or Visual Studio 2008 using .NET 3.0 and 3.5. In this instance, it doesn't matter which tool or runtime is selected because there isn't really a dependency on the runtime as you will only be making modifications to the web application's Web.Config file. In this example, Visual Studio 2008 using the .NET Framework 3.0 is used.

When you click the Create Solution button, you are presented with a dialog box (Figure B.2) in which you must select the scope of your SharePoint feature. Because the Web.Config file will need to be modified, you must scope the feature to the web application level.

FIGURE B.2   Configuring the feature's scope.

Using Visual Studio

After you have created your Visual Studio solution and project files with STSDev, you can now begin to create your feature. As a brief overview, you should understand the files and directory structures that get created.

Figure B.3 shows the Visual Studio project that will be modified as it appears in the Visual Studio Solution Explorer.

Beginning in the root directory of the project, there is a file called FeatureReceiver.cs. This is where your feature's code will be created. Listing B.1 shows this nice little class, which is already preconfigured so that you can easily begin coding your feature.

LISTING B.1   FeatureReceiver.cs

```
using System;
using System.Web;
using System.Web.UI;
using System.Web.UI.WebControls;
using System.Web.UI.WebControls.WebParts;

using Microsoft.SharePoint;
using Microsoft.SharePoint.WebControls;
using Microsoft.SharePoint.WebPartPages;
```

```csharp
using Microsoft.SharePoint.Navigation;
using Microsoft.SharePoint.Administration;

namespace ThreeFive {
  public class FeatureReceiver : SPFeatureReceiver {

    public override void FeatureActivated(SPFeatureReceiverProperties properties) {
        /* no op */
    }

    public override void FeatureDeactivating(SPFeatureReceiverProperties
➥properties) {
        /* no op */
    }

    public override void FeatureInstalled(SPFeatureReceiverProperties properties) {
        /* no op */
    }
    public override void FeatureUninstalling(SPFeatureReceiverProperties
➥properties) {
        /* no op */
    }
  }
}
```

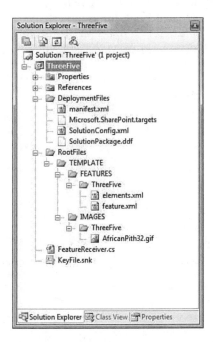

FIGURE B.3   Viewing the SharePoint feature in Visual Studio.

The code behind the class is simple: There are four events that you can write code against, which are self-explanatory: `FeatureActivated`, `FeatureDeactivating`, `FeatureInstalled`, and `FeatureUninstalling`.

In the example in this chapter, you will only write code in the `FeatureActivated` and `FeatureDeactivating` events, which will fire as a result of the feature being activated or deactivated.

Moving up the Solution Explorer tree (Figure B.3), you will notice a directory called RootFiles. Inside of this directory, a representation of the "12 hive" has been created to represent how your feature's files will be deployed to SharePoint.

> **NOTE**
>
> Note that "12 hive" is a term that is used to describe the directory structure located at C:\Program Files\Common Files\Microsoft Shared\web server extensions\12 directory of your SharePoint web servers.

The first subdirectory structure is named Template\Features\ThreeFive. This represents the directory that will get created on the SharePoint web servers that will be used to house your feature. You need to ensure that this name is unique and doesn't already exist in this directory on your SharePoint web servers (unless, of course, you want to update that feature).

Two files are created inside of the Template\Features\ThreeFive directory: Elements.xml and Feature.xml. These files are used to describe the feature itself. Most important, you need to modify the Feature.xml file so that it provides a title and description that the end users (or, in this case, the administrators) will see on the SharePoint site. Listing B.2 illustrates the Feature.xml file.

LISTING B.2   Feature.xml

```
<?xml version="1.0" encoding="utf-8"?>
<!--Created by STSDEV at 5/6/2008 11:16:07 PM-->
<Feature
  Id="16FED0DD-0805-447B-8EBF-EB7EC4E46871"
  Title=".NET Framework 3.5"
  Description="Installs the .NET Framework 3.5 for the web application"
  Version="1.0.0.0"
  Scope="WebApplication"
  Hidden="false"
  ImageUrl="ThreeFive\AfricanPith32.gif"
  ReceiverAssembly="ThreeFive, Version=1.0.0.0, Culture=neutral,
 PublicKeyToken=f2a4959f56856b94"
  ReceiverClass="ThreeFive.FeatureReceiver"
 xmlns="http://schemas.microsoft.com/sharepoint/">
```

```
<ElementManifests>
  <ElementManifest
    Location="elements.xml" />
</ElementManifests>
</Feature>
```

The only modification that was made to this file was to the Title and Description attributes of the Feature element to provide a better description of the feature itself.

After you have configured the Feature.xml file, you are almost ready to begin coding your feature. There is one more directory that has been created and associated with your project called DeploymentFiles. This directory contains the files that will be used by Visual Studio to package the feature into a SharePoint solution for deployment. STSDev creates an XML file inside of the DeploymentFiles directory called SolutionConfig.xml that will be used by Visual Studio to help create the SharePoint solution. Listing B.3 illustrates this file.

LISTING B.3   SolutionConfig.xml

```
<?xml version="1.0" encoding="utf-8"?>
<!--Created by STSDEV at 5/6/2008 11:16:07 PM-->
<Solution>
  <SolutionId>0B697BF6-F95B-4AF3-8B23-24E34EF77F29</SolutionId>
  <SolutionName>ThreeFive</SolutionName>
  <ResetWebServer>True</ResetWebServer>
  <AssemblyDeployment>True</AssemblyDeployment>
  <SafeControlSettings>False</SafeControlSettings>
  <CasPermissions>False</CasPermissions>
  <!--Assembly files-->
  <Assemblies>
    <Assembly Location="ThreeFive.dll" DeploymentTarget="GlobalAssemblyCache">
      <SafeControls>
        <SafeControl Assembly="ThreeFive, Version=1.0.0.0, Culture=neutral,
➥PublicKeyToken=f2a4959f56856b94" Namespace="ThreeFive" TypeName="*"
➥Safe="True" />
      </SafeControls>
    </Assembly>
  </Assemblies>
</Solution>
```

The SolutionConfig.xml file defines several things that you can trigger as a result of your solution being deployed to SharePoint. For example, you can see in Listing B.3 that the solution name has been configured to read "ThreeFive" and the ResetWebServer attribute is set to `True`, which will force an `IISReset` to occur when you deploy your SharePoint solution.

As you can see, the STSDev tool will save you a lot of time and effort in creating your SharePoint solution and properly configuring Visual Studio for developing a feature. In the next section, you learn how to develop a feature receiver that allows SharePoint to use the .NET Framework 3.5 and ASP.NET 3.5 AJAX.

Creating the Feature Receiver

Creating the event receiver is a simple process if you focus on what you are trying to accomplish as opposed to the length of the code that is described in this section. Fundamentally, you need to code against two events of the feature receiver: `FeatureActivated` and `FeatureDeactivating`.

When the feature is activated, you want to modify the Web.Config file to use the .NET Framework 3.5 and when the feature is deactivated, you want to remove those modifications and restore the Web.Config file to its original state.

Before diving into the complete code listing (later in this section), it is important to understand what is happening in the code. All of the modifications that are going to be made to the Web.Config file are represented by a C# structure called `ModificationEntry`, which is illustrated in Listing B.4.

LISTING B.4   The `ModificationEntry` Structure

```
        /// <summary>
        /// Struct that represents the modification that is being made to the
➥Web.Config
        /// </summary>
        private struct ModificationEntry
        {
            //members
            public string Name;
            public string XPath;
            public string Value;


            //constructor
            public ModificationEntry(string Name,
                                     string XPath,
                                     string Value)
            {
                this.Name = Name;
                this.XPath = XPath;
                this.Value = Value;
```

```
        }
    }
```

The `ModificationEntry` structure contains three properties, which are described in the following list:

- ▶ **Name**—The name of the section or section group that's being modified

- ▶ **XPath**—The location in which the modification will be made

- ▶ **Value**—The new text that will replace what's currently defined in the Web.Config file

The `ModificationEntry` structure represents the modification that will be made to the Web.Config file, and the `CreateChildNode` method will make the update to the Web.Config file itself by accepting a `ModificationEntry` structure as a parameter. Listing B.5 illustrates the `CreateChildNode` method.

LISTING B.5   CreateChildNode Method

```
        /// <summary>
        /// Creates a child node in the Web.Config
        /// </summary>
        /// <param name="modEntry">Modification that is being made
(TypeOf ModificationEntry Struct</param>
        /// <returns></returns>
        private SPWebConfigModification CreateChildNode(ModificationEntry modEntry)
        {
            // create and return SPWebConfigModification object
            SPWebConfigModification modification;
            modification = new SPWebConfigModification(modEntry.Name,
➥modEntry.XPath);
            modification.Owner = "Unleashed.ThreeFive";
            modification.Sequence = 0;
            modification.Type =
➥SPWebConfigModification.SPWebConfigModificationType.EnsureChildNode;
            modification.Value = modEntry.Value;
            return modification;
        }
```

The `CreateChildNode` method will create an instance of the `SPWebConfigModification` class from the SharePoint object model and then configure it so that the defined modification (passed in as a parameter) can be made to the Web.Config file.

These two sections of code are crucial as they are core to making the modifications to the Web.Config file itself.

Listing B.6 provides a complete listing of the FeatureReceiver.cs file.

LISTING B.6   FeatureReceiver.cs

```csharp
using System;
using System.Web;
using System.Web.UI;
using System.Web.UI.WebControls;
using System.Web.UI.WebControls.WebParts;

using Microsoft.SharePoint;
using Microsoft.SharePoint.WebControls;
using Microsoft.SharePoint.WebPartPages;
using Microsoft.SharePoint.Navigation;
using Microsoft.SharePoint.Administration;

namespace ThreeFive
{
    public class FeatureReceiver : SPFeatureReceiver
    {


        /// <summary>
        /// Executes when the feature is activated (i.e. the user clicks "activate")
        /// </summary>
        /// <param name="properties"></param>
        public override void FeatureActivated(SPFeatureReceiverProperties properties)
        {
            SPWebApplication app = (SPWebApplication)properties.Feature.Parent;
            foreach (ModificationEntry m in Entries)
            {
                app.WebConfigModifications.Add(
                  CreateChildNode(m)
                );
            }
            app.WebService.ApplyWebConfigModifications();
        }


        /// <summary>
        /// Executes when the feature is deactivated (i.e. the user clicks
➥"deactivate")
        /// </summary>
        /// <param name="properties"></param>
        public override void FeatureDeactivating(SPFeatureReceiverProperties
➥properties)
        {
            SPWebApplication app = (SPWebApplication)properties.Feature.Parent;
            foreach (ModificationEntry m in Entries)
```

```
            {
                app.WebConfigModifications.Remove(CreateChildNode(m));
            }
            app.WebService.ApplyWebConfigModifications();
        }


        /// <summary>
        /// NOT USED--Executes when the feature is installed
        /// </summary>
        /// <param name="properties"></param>
        public override void FeatureInstalled(SPFeatureReceiverProperties
➥properties) { }


        /// <summary>
        /// NOT USED--Executes when the feature is uninstalling
        /// </summary>
        /// <param name="properties"></param>
        public override void FeatureUninstalling(SPFeatureReceiverProperties
➥properties) { }


        /// <summary>
        /// Struct that represents the modification that is being made to the
➥Web.Config
        /// </summary>
        private struct ModificationEntry
        {
            //members
            public string Name;
            public string XPath;
            public string Value;


            //constructor
            public ModificationEntry(string Name,
                                     string XPath,
                                     string Value)
            {
                this.Name = Name;
                this.XPath = XPath;
                this.Value = Value;


            }
        }


        /// <summary>
        /// Creates a child node in the Web.Config
```

LISTING B.6   Continued

```
        /// </summary>
        /// <param name="modEntry">Modification that is being made
➥(TypeOf ModificationEntry Struct</param>
        /// <returns></returns>
        private SPWebConfigModification CreateChildNode(ModificationEntry modEntry)
        {
            // create and return SPWebConfigModification object
            SPWebConfigModification modification;
            modification = new SPWebConfigModification(modEntry.Name,
➥modEntry.XPath);
            modification.Owner = "Unleashed.ThreeFive";
            modification.Sequence = 0;
            modification.Type =
➥SPWebConfigModification.SPWebConfigModificationType.EnsureChildNode;
            modification.Value = modEntry.Value;
            return modification;
        }

        /// <summary>
        /// Array that contains the modifications to Web.Config.
        /// This will be used to both add and remove
        /// modifications when the feature is activated and deactivated
        /// </summary>
        private ModificationEntry[] Entries = {
            new ModificationEntry(
                "sectionGroup[@name='system.web.extensions']",
                "configuration/configSections",
                @"<sectionGroup name=""system.web.extensions""
➥type=""System.Web.Configuration.SystemWebExtensionsSectionGroup,
➥System.Web.Extensions, Version=3.5.0.0, Culture=neutral,
➥PublicKeyToken=31BF3856AD364E35""></sectionGroup>"),

            new ModificationEntry(
                "sectionGroup[@name='scripting']",
                "configuration/configSections/sectionGroup[@name=
➥'system.web.extensions']",@"<sectionGroup name=""scripting""
➥type=""System.Web.Configuration.ScriptingSectionGroup, System.Web.Extensions,
➥Version=3.5.0.0, Culture=neutral, PublicKeyToken=31BF3856AD364E35"">
➥</sectionGroup>"),

            new ModificationEntry(
                "section[@name='scriptResourceHandler']",
                "configuration/configSections/sectionGroup[@name=
➥'system.web.extensions']/sectionGroup[@name='scripting']",
                @"<section name=""scriptResourceHandler""
➥type=""System.Web.Configuration.ScriptingScriptResourceHandlerSection,
```

```
➥System.Web.Extensions, Version=3.5.0.0, Culture=neutral,
➥PublicKeyToken=31BF3856AD364E35"" requirePermission=""false""
➥allowDefinition=""MachineToApplication""/>"),

            new ModificationEntry(
                "sectionGroup[@name='webServices']",
                "configuration/configSections/sectionGroup[@name=
➥'system.web.extensions']/sectionGroup[@name='scripting']",
                @"<sectionGroup name=""webServices""
➥type=""System.Web.Configuration.ScriptingWebServicesSectionGroup,
➥System.Web.Extensions, Version=3.5.0.0, Culture=neutral,
➥PublicKeyToken=31BF3856AD364E35""></sectionGroup>"),

            new ModificationEntry(
                "section[@name='jsonSerialization']",
                "configuration/configSections/sectionGroup[@name=
➥'system.web.extensions']/sectionGroup[@name='scripting']/sectionGroup
➥[@name='WebServices']"
                @"<section name=""jsonSerialization""
➥type=""System.Web.Configuration.ScriptingJsonSerializationSection,
➥System.Web.Extensions,Version=3.5.0.0, Culture=neutral,
➥PublicKeyToken=31BF3856AD364E35"" requirePermission=""false""
➥allowDefinition=""Everywhere"" />" ),

            new ModificationEntry(
                "section[@name='profileService']",
                "configuration/configSections/sectionGroup[@name=
➥'system.web.extensions']/sectionGroup[@name='scripting']/sectionGroup
➥[@name='WebServices']"
                @"<section name=""profileService""
➥type=""System.Web.Configuration.ScriptingProfileServiceSection,
➥System.Web.Extensions, Version=3.5.0.0, Culture=neutral,
➥PublicKeyToken=31BF3856AD364E35"" requirePermission=""false""
➥allowDefinition=""MachineToApplication"" />"),

            new ModificationEntry(
                "section[@name='authenticationService']",
                "configuration/configSections/sectionGroup[@name=
➥'system.web.extensions']/sectionGroup[@name='scripting']
➥/sectionGroup[@name='WebServices']"
                @"<section name=""authenticationService""
➥"type=""System.Web.Configuration.ScriptingAuthenticationServiceSection,
➥System.Web.Extensions, Version=3.5.0.0, Culture=neutral,
➥PublicKeyToken=31BF3856AD364E35"" requirePermission=""false""
➥allowDefinition=""MachineToApplication"" />"),

            new ModificationEntry(
                "section[@name='roleService']",
                "configuration/configSections/sectionGroup[@name=
➥'system.web.extensions']/sectionGroup[@name='scripting']
```

LISTING B.6   Continued

```
➡/sectionGroup[[@name='WebServices']]"
            @"<section name=""roleService""
➡type=""System.Web.Configuration.ScriptingRoleServiceSection,
➡System.Web.Extensions, Version=3.5.0.0, Culture=neutral,
➡PublicKeyToken=31BF3856AD364E35"" requirePermission=""false""
➡allowDefinition=""MachineToApplication"" />"),

                new ModificationEntry(
                    "pages",
                "configuration/system.web",
                @"<pages />"),

                new ModificationEntry(
                    "controls",
                "configuration/system.web/pages",
                @"<controls />"),

                new ModificationEntry(
                    "add[@namespace='System.Web.UI']",
                "configuration/system.web/pages/controls",
                @"<add tagPrefix=""asp"" namespace=""System.Web.UI""
➡assembly=""System.Web.Extensions, Version=3.5.0.0, Culture=neutral,
➡PublicKeyToken=31BF3856AD364E35""/>"),

                new ModificationEntry(
                    "add[@namespace='System.Web.UI.WebControls']",
                "configuration/system.web/pages/controls",
                @"<add tagPrefix=""asp"" namespace=""System.Web.UI.WebControls""
➡assembly=""System.Web.Extensions, Version=3.5.0.0, Culture=neutral,
➡PublicKeyToken=31BF3856AD364E35""/>"),

                new ModificationEntry(
                    "add[@assembly='System.Core, Version=3.5.0.0, Culture=neutral,
➡PublicKeyToken=B77A5C561934E089']",
                "configuration/system.web/compilation/assemblies",
                @"<add assembly=""System.Core, Version=3.5.0.0, Culture=neutral,
➡PublicKeyToken=B77A5C561934E089""/>"),

                new ModificationEntry(
                    "add[@assembly='System.Web.Extensions, Version=3.5.0.0,
➡Culture=neutral, PublicKeyToken=31BF3856AD364E35']",
                "configuration/system.web/compilation/assemblies",
                @"<add assembly=""System.Web.Extensions, Version=3.5.0.0,
➡Culture=neutral, PublicKeyToken=31BF3856AD364E35""/> "),

                new ModificationEntry(
                    "add[@assembly='System.Data.DataSetExtensions, Version=3.5.0.0,
➡Culture=neutral, PublicKeyToken=B77A5C561934E089']",
```

```
                "configuration/system.web/compilation/assemblies",
                @"<add assembly=""System.Data.DataSetExtensions, Version=3.5.0.0,
➥Culture=neutral, PublicKeyToken=B77A5C561934E089""/>"),

            new ModificationEntry(
                "add[@assembly='System.Xml.Linq, Version=3.5.0.0, Culture=neutral,
➥PublicKeyToken=B77A5C561934E089']",
                "configuration/system.web/compilation/assemblies",
                @"<add assembly=""System.Xml.Linq, Version=3.5.0.0, Culture=neutral,
➥PublicKeyToken=B77A5C561934E089""/>"),

            new ModificationEntry(
                "remove[@path='*.asmx']",
                "configuration/system.web/httpHandlers",
                @"<remove verb=""*"" path=""*.asmx""/> "),

            new ModificationEntry(
                "add[@path='*.asmx']",
                "configuration/system.web/httpHandlers",
                @"<add verb=""*"" path=""*.asmx"" validate=""false""
➥type=""System.Web.Script.Services.ScriptHandlerFactory, System.Web.Extensions,
➥Version=3.5.0.0, Culture=neutral, PublicKeyToken=31BF3856AD364E35""/>"),

            new ModificationEntry(
                "add[@path='*_AppService.axd']",
                "configuration/system.web/httpHandlers",
                @"<add verb=""*"" path=""*_AppService.axd"" validate=""false""
➥type=""System.Web.Script.Services.ScriptHandlerFactory, System.Web.Extensions,
➥Version=3.5.0.0, Culture=neutral, PublicKeyToken=31BF3856AD364E35""/>"),

            new ModificationEntry(
                "add[@path='ScriptResource.axd']",
                "configuration/system.web/httpHandlers",
                @"<add verb=""GET,HEAD"" path=""ScriptResource.axd""
➥type=""System.Web.Handlers.ScriptResourceHandler, System.Web.Extensions,
➥Version=3.5.0.0, Culture=neutral, PublicKeyToken=31BF3856AD364E35""
➥validate=""false""/>"),

            new ModificationEntry(
                "add[@name='ScriptModule']",
                "configuration/system.web/httpModules",
                @"<add name=""ScriptModule"" type=""System.Web.Handlers.ScriptModule,
➥System.Web.Extensions, Version=3.5.0.0, Culture=neutral,
➥PublicKeyToken=31BF3856AD364E35""/>"),
```

LISTING B.6   Continued

```
            new ModificationEntry(
                "SafeControl[@Assembly='System.Web.Extensions, Version=3.5.0.0,
➥Culture=neutral, PublicKeyToken=31bf3856ad364e35']
➥[@Namespace='System.Web.UI'][@TypeName='*']",
                "configuration/SharePoint/SafeControls",
                @"<SafeControl Assembly=""System.Web.Extensions, Version=3.5.0.0,
➥Culture=neutral, PublicKeyToken=31bf3856ad364e35""
➥Namespace=""System.Web.UI"" TypeName=""*"" Safe=""True"" />"),

            new ModificationEntry(
                "system.web.extensions",
                "configuration",
                @"<system.web.extensions />"),

            new ModificationEntry(
                "scripting",
                "configuration/system.web.extensions",
                @"<scripting />"),

            new ModificationEntry(
                "webServices",
                "configuration/system.web.extensions/scripting",
                @"<webServices />"),

            new ModificationEntry(
                "system.webServer",
                "configuration",
                @"<system.webServer />"),

            new ModificationEntry(
                "modules",
                "configuration/system.webServer",
                @"<modules />"),

            new ModificationEntry(
                "handlers",
                "configuration/system.webServer",
                @"<handlers />"),

            new ModificationEntry(
                "validation[@validateIntegratedModeConfiguration='false']",
                "configuration/system.webServer",
                @"<validation validateIntegratedModeConfiguration=""false""/>"),

            new ModificationEntry(
                "remove[@name='ScriptModule']",
```

```
                "configuration/system.webServer/modules",
                @"<remove name=""ScriptModule"" />"),

        new ModificationEntry(
            "add[@name='ScriptModule']",
            "configuration/system.webServer/modules",
            @"<add name=""ScriptModule"" preCondition=""managedHandler""
➥type=""System.Web.Handlers.ScriptModule, System.Web.Extensions,
➥Version=3.5.0.0, Culture=neutral, PublicKeyToken=31BF3856AD364E35""/>"),

            new ModificationEntry(
                "remove[@name='WebServiceHandlerFactory-Integrated']",
                "configuration/system.webServer/handlers",
                @"<remove name=""WebServiceHandlerFactory-Integrated"" />"),

        new ModificationEntry(
            "remove[@name='ScriptHandlerFactory']",
            "configuration/system.webServer/handlers",
            @"<remove name=""ScriptHandlerFactory"" />"),

        new ModificationEntry(
            "remove[@name='ScriptHandlerFactoryAppServices']",
            "configuration/system.webServer/handlers",
            @"<remove name=""ScriptHandlerFactoryAppServices"" />"),

        new ModificationEntry(
            "remove[@name='ScriptResource']",
            "configuration/system.webServer/handlers",
            @"<remove name=""ScriptResource"" />"),

        new ModificationEntry(
            "add[@name='ScriptHandlerFactory']",
            "configuration/system.webServer/handlers",
            @"<add name=""ScriptHandlerFactory"" verb=""*"" path=""*.asmx""
➥preCondition=""integratedMode""
➥type=""System.Web.Script.Services.ScriptHandlerFactory, System.Web.Extensions,
➥Version=3.5.0.0, Culture=neutral, PublicKeyToken=31BF3856AD364E35""/>"),

            new ModificationEntry(
                "add[@name='ScriptHandlerFactoryAppServices']",
                "configuration/system.webServer/handlers",
                @"<add name=""ScriptHandlerFactoryAppServices"" verb=""*""
➥path=""*_AppService.axd"" preCondition=""integratedMode""
➥type=""System.Web.Script.Services.ScriptHandlerFactory, System.Web.Extensions,
➥Version=3.5.0.0, Culture=neutral, PublicKeyToken=31BF3856AD364E35""/>"),
```

LISTING B.6   Continued

```
                new ModificationEntry(
                    "add[@name='ScriptResource']",
                    "configuration/system.webServer/handlers",
                    @"<add name=""ScriptResource"" preCondition=""integratedMode""
➥verb=""GET,HEAD"" path=""ScriptResource.axd""
➥type=""System.Web.Handlers.ScriptResourceHandler, System.Web.Extensions,
➥Version=3.5.0.0, Culture=neutral, PublicKeyToken=31BF3856AD364E35"" />"),

        };
    }
}
```

After grasping the core concepts of this code (Listings B.4 and B.5), it is quite simple. There is an array of `ModificationEntry` objects that is defined that contains all of the modifications that will be made to the Web.Config file in the order that you would like to make them (these are also described in the previous chapter). Other than the length of the array definition, it is quite a simple piece of code.

The actual modifications to the Web.Config file are made using the `FeatureActivated` and `FeatureDeactivating` events of the `FeatureReceiver` class. In the `FeatureActivated` event, the array is looped and each setting is added as a modification to the Web.Config file. Conversely, on the `FeatureDeactivating` event, the array is looped and each setting is removed from the Web.Config file.

Creating a feature to make modifications to the Web.Config file is quite simple; however, because of the number of modifications that need to be made to enable the .NET Framework 3.5, the length of the code makes it seem more complex than it actually is.

Deploying the Solution to SharePoint

After you have built your feature and solution using Visual Studio, you need to deploy it to a SharePoint server so that you can test/debug. Follow these steps to deploy a solution and a feature:

1. Compile the solution with Visual Studio.
2. Run STSADM.EXE to register the solution.
3. Deploy the solution using SharePoint Central Management.
4. Activate the feature.

Compiling the Solution

Before you compile the solution, you should pay close attention to a few files because they directly affect how your solution will be built, deployed, and managed. These files aid in the process of building the SharePoint solution that is used to deploy the feature. The first file that you should examine is named SolutionConfig.xml and is shown in Listing B.7.

LISTING B.7   SolutionConfig.xml

```xml
<?xml version="1.0" encoding="utf-8"?>
<!--Created by STSDEV at 5/8/2008 9:01:22 PM-->
<Solution>
  <SolutionId>A12CB189-2529-4C64-8BE9-61CCC2DDC0AF</SolutionId>
  <SolutionName>ThreeFive</SolutionName>
  <ResetWebServer>True</ResetWebServer>
  <AssemblyDeployment>True</AssemblyDeployment>
  <SafeControlSettings>False</SafeControlSettings>
  <CasPermissions>False</CasPermissions>
  <!--Assembly files-->
  <Assemblies>
    <Assembly Location="ThreeFive.dll" DeploymentTarget="GlobalAssemblyCache">
      <SafeControls>
        <SafeControl Assembly="ThreeFive, Version=1.0.0.0,
Culture=neutral, PublicKeyToken=1ad5be45b2e75f7f"
Namespace="ThreeFive" TypeName="*" Safe="True" />
      </SafeControls>
    </Assembly>
  </Assemblies>
</Solution>
```

SolutionConfig.xml, as its name suggests, is the configuration file that will be used to configure *how* (or what will happen when) your SharePoint solution file is deployed. The elements of SolutionConfig.xml are described in Table B.1.

TABLE B.1   SolutionConfig Elements

Element	Description
SolutionId	The unique identifier (a GUID) for the solution package. This GUID will be used by SharePoint to identify the solution.
SolutionName	The name of the solution. This is what will be displayed in SharePoint on the Solution Management page. It defaults to the name of your project.
ResetWebServer	The Boolean that will determine if IIS gets reset after the solution is deployed. Its default value is True.
AssemblyDeployment	The Boolean that determines if there are assemblies that need to be deployed to the global assembly cache (GAC). If there is an assembly deployment and the value of this element is True, you need to ensure that the Assembly element is properly configured in the Assemblies element hierarchy. The Assembly element is configured to only reflect the first project in the solution that was created by STSDev.

TABLE B.1   Continued

Element	Description
SafeControlSettings	The Boolean that determines if there are controls (usually Web Parts) that need to be configured in the Web.Config file. If there is a Web Part that is getting deployed and the value of this element is True, you need to ensure that the SafeControls element is properly configured in the Assemblies element hierarchy. The SafeControls element is configured to only reflect the first project in the solution that was created by STSDev.
CasPermissions	The Boolean that determines if there are code access permissions that are being configured on the assembly.
Assemblies	The Assemblies element hierarchy allows you to configure the assemblies and safe controls that will be deployed in your project, using the Assembly and SafeControls attributes, respectively.

After you compile your solution, several things are going to happen. A few extra steps are going to be executed at compile time that will build the SharePoint package files (a .cab file and a .wsp file). First, a cabinet file will be created with instructions defined by the SolutionPackage.ddf file, which was initially created by STSDev. SolutionPackage.ddf is illustrated in Listing B.8.

LISTING B.8   SolutionPackage.ddf

```
; Generated by STSDEV


.OPTION EXPLICIT
.Set CabinetNameTemplate=ThreeFive.wsp
.set DiskDirectoryTemplate=CDROM
.Set CompressionType=MSZIP
.Set UniqueFiles=off
.Set Cabinet=on
.Set DiskDirectory1=DeploymentFiles

;*** Solution manifest
DeploymentFiles\manifest.xml

;*** Assembly files
bin/debug/ThreeFive.dll

;*** add files for ThreeFive feature
```

```
.Set DestinationDir=ThreeFive
RootFiles\TEMPLATE\FEATURES\ThreeFive\elements.xml
RootFiles\TEMPLATE\FEATURES\ThreeFive\feature.xml



;**********************************
;*** Begin TemplateFiles section ***
;**********************************


.Set DestinationDir=IMAGES\ThreeFive
RootFiles\TEMPLATE\IMAGES\ThreeFive\AfricanPith32.gif
```

This file is actually loaded into the C:\Windows\System32\MakeCab.Exe file during your project's compile time and a CAB and WSP file are created using the following command (which is an excerpt from the compiler's output window in Visual Studio 2008):

```
"C:\Windows\System32\makecab.exe" /F DeploymentFiles\SolutionPackage.ddf /D
 CabinetNameTemplate=ThreeFive.wsp
```

As mentioned earlier, several steps get executed during compile time of your project that was configured with STSDev. These steps are defined in the Microsoft.SharePoint.targets file, which is in the DeploymentFiles directory of your project and is described in Listing B.9.

LISTING B.9   Microsoft.SharePoint.targets

```
<?xml version="1.0" encoding="utf-8" ?>



<Project DefaultTargets="DebugBuild"
➥xmlns="http://schemas.microsoft.com/developer/msbuild/2003">

  <PropertyGroup>
    <PackageName>ThreeFive.wsp</PackageName>
    <PackageFile>ThreeFive.wsp</PackageFile>
    <TargetUrl>http://litwareinc.com</TargetUrl>
    <ProjectDeploymentFilesFolder>DeploymentFiles</ProjectDeploymentFilesFolder>
    <ProjectRootFilesFolder>RootFiles</ProjectRootFilesFolder>
    <WssRootFilesFolder>"$(ProgramFiles)\Common Files\Microsoft Shared\
➥web server extensions\12"</WssRootFilesFolder>
    <MAKECAB>"C:\Windows\System32\makecab.exe"</MAKECAB>
    <STSADM>"$(ProgramFiles)\Common Files\Microsoft Shared\web server
➥extensions\12\bin\stsadm.exe"</STSADM>
    <STSDEV>"C:\Documents and Settings\Administrator\Desktop\stsdev\stsdev.exe"
➥</STSDEV>
  </PropertyGroup>
```

LISTING B.9   Continued

```
<Target Name="DebugBuild">
  <Message Text="Refreshing Deployment Files..." Importance="high" />
  <Exec Command="$(STSDEV) /refresh $(TargetName) $(SolutionDir)"
➥ContinueOnError="true" />
  <Message Text="Deleting Solution Package File..." Importance="high" />
  <Delete Files="$(ProjectDeploymentFilesFolder)\$(PackageFile)"
➥ContinueOnError="true" />
  <Message Text="Building Solution Package (Debug Version)" Importance="high" />
  <Exec Command="$(MAKECAB) /F $(ProjectDeploymentFilesFolder)\SolutionPackage.ddf
➥/D CabinetNameTemplate=$(PackageFile)" ContinueOnError="false" />
  <!--Added 2/6/08 DMann-->
  <Message Text="" Importance="high" />
  <Message Text="Copying WSP file to CAB" Importance="high" />
  <Delete Files="$(ProjectDeploymentFilesFolder)\$(PackageFile).cab"
➥ContinueOnError="true" />
  <Copy SourceFiles="$(ProjectDeploymentFilesFolder)\$(PackageFile)"
➥DestinationFiles="$(ProjectDeploymentFilesFolder)\$(PackageFile).cab"
➥SkipUnchangedFiles="false" />
  <!--End of 2/6/08 Add-->
  <Message Text="" Importance="high" />
</Target>

<Target Name="DebugInstall" DependsOnTargets="DebugBuild">
  <Message Text="Installing Solution..." Importance="high" />
  <Exec Command="$(STSADM) -o addsolution -filename
➥$(ProjectDeploymentFilesFolder)\$(PackageFile)" ContinueOnError="true" />
  <Exec Command="$(STSADM) -o execadmsvcjobs" />
  <Message Text="" Importance="high" />
</Target>

<Target Name="DebugDeploy" DependsOnTargets="DebugInstall">
  <Message Text="Deploying Solution..." Importance="high" />
  <Exec Command="$(STSADM) -o deploysolution -name $(PackageName) -immediate
➥-allowgacdeployment" />
  <Exec Command="$(STSADM) -o execadmsvcjobs" />
  <Message Text="" Importance="high" />
</Target>

<Target Name="DebugRedeploy" >
  <Message Text="" Importance="high" />
  <Message Text="Starting sequence of Retract/Delete/Build/Install/Deploy"
➥Importance="high" />
  <CallTarget Targets="DebugRetract" />
  <CallTarget Targets="DebugDelete" />
  <CallTarget Targets="DebugBuild" />
```

```xml
    <CallTarget Targets="DebugInstall" />
    <CallTarget Targets="DebugDeploy" />
    <CallTarget Targets="DebugDeploy" />
    <Message Text="" Importance="high" />
  </Target>

  <Target Name="DebugUpgrade" DependsOnTargets="DebugBuild">
    <Message Text="Updating solution" Importance="high" />
    <Exec Command="$(STSADM) -o upgradesolution -name $(PackageName) -filename
➥$(ProjectDeploymentFilesFolder)\$(PackageFile) -local -allowgacdeployment" />
    <Exec Command="$(STSADM) -o execadmsvcjobs" />
    <Message Text="" Importance="high" />
  </Target>

  <Target Name="DebugQuickCopy" >
    <Message Text="Copying Root Files to WSS system folder" />
    <Copy SourceFiles="$(ProjectRootFilesFolder)\*"
➥DestinationFolder="$(WssRootFilesFolder)" SkipUnchangedFiles="true" />
    <Message Text="" Importance="high" />
  </Target>

  <Target Name="DebugRetract" >
    <Message Text="Retracting Solution" />
    <Exec Command="$(STSADM) -o retractsolution -name $(PackageName) -immediate"
➥ContinueOnError="true" />
    <Exec Command="$(STSADM) -o execadmsvcjobs" />
    <Message Text="" Importance="high" />
  </Target>

  <Target Name="DebugDelete" DependsOnTargets="DebugRetract">
    <Message Text="Deleting Solution Package from Farm Solution Package Store" />
    <Exec Command="$(STSADM) -o deletesolution -name $(PackageName)"
➥ContinueOnError="true" />
    <Exec Command="$(STSADM) -o execadmsvcjobs" />
    <Message Text="" Importance="high" />
  </Target>

  <Target Name="ReleaseBuild" >
    <Message Text="Deleting Pacakge File..." Importance="high" />
    <Delete Files="$(ProjectDeploymentFilesFolder)\SolutionPackage.ddf"
➥ContinueOnError="true" />
    <Message Text="Building Cab File (Release Version)" Importance="high" />
    <Exec Command="$(MAKECAB) /F $(ProjectDeploymentFilesFolder)\SolutionPackage.ddf
➥/D CabinetNameTemplate=$(PackageFile)" ContinueOnError="false" />
    <!--Added 2/6/08 DMann-->
    <Message Text="" Importance="high" />
```

LISTING B.9   Continued

```
  <Message Text="Copying WSP file to CAB" Importance="high" />
  <Delete Files="$(ProjectDeploymentFilesFolder)\$(PackageFile).cab"
➥ContinueOnError="true" />
  <Copy SourceFiles="$(ProjectDeploymentFilesFolder)\$(PackageFile)"
➥DestinationFiles="$(ProjectDeploymentFilesFolder)\$(PackageFile).cab"
➥SkipUnchangedFiles="false" />
  <!--End of 2/6/08 Add-->
  <Message Text="" Importance="high" />
</Target>
</Project>
```

Microsoft.SharePoint.targets describes the solution itself, as well as the steps that execute during a compile of the project. In the first element section, <PropertyGroup>, the SharePoint solution package is described, as well as some initial definitions for the executable file locations that will be invoked by the compiler.

Next, several <Target> elements are used to describe the steps that will execute during several different build scenarios (for example, DebugBuild, DebugInstall, ReleaseBuild, ReleaseInstall) and their dependencies. This file is crucial because you can customize the steps that get executed during compile time so that the build process fits into your team's defined build process.

Running STSADM.EXE to Register the Solution

After your Visual Studio project has been compiled (and it finishes without errors, of course), you can now deploy the .wsp file to SharePoint. This can be done with the STSADM.EXE command-line utility that is included with SharePoint 2007. Figure B.4 illustrates using STSADM.EXE to deploy the solution to your SharePoint farm.

FIGURE B.4   Using STSADM.EXE to deploy the solution.

After you successfully deploy the solution file (the .wsp), it is made available to you on the Solution Management page, which is found on the Operations tab of SharePoint Central Administration.

Deploying the Solution Using SharePoint Central Management

Figure B.5 illustrates the Solution Management page.

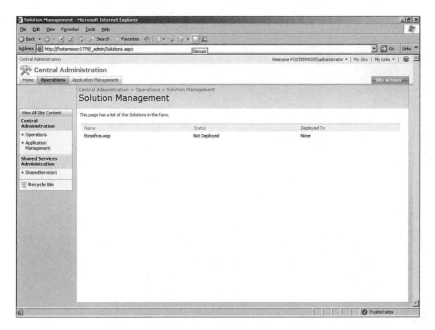

FIGURE B.5   Solution Management page.

Notice that the solution is showing up on the Solution Management page, but its status is Not Deployed. This means that you have successfully registered the solution and now you must deploy it. You can start the deployment process by clicking on the solution name (ThreeFive.wsp). This takes you to the Solution Properties page of the ThreeFive.wsp solution, which is illustrated in Figure B.6.

You can now deploy the solution by clicking on the Deploy Solution button at the top of the page. This directs you to a page that will help you deploy your solution either immediately or schedule a date and time to deploy your solution.

In this example, the solution will be deployed immediately, but you might want to schedule a deployment during off-peak usage time as deploying this solution restarts IIS because the <RestartWebServer> element in the SolutionConfig.xml file (Listing B.7) is set to True, which means that your users will be affected by deploying this solution. Figure B.7 shows the Deploy Solution page that you can use to either deploy your solution immediately or schedule a deployment for off-peak hours.

When you click the OK button in Figure B.7, the solution will be deployed and you will be redirected to the Solution Management page, as shown in Figure B.8. Notice that the solution is now showing a status of Deployed.

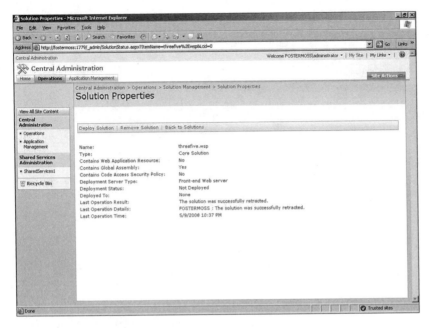

FIGURE B.6   Solution Properties for the ThreeFive.wsp solution.

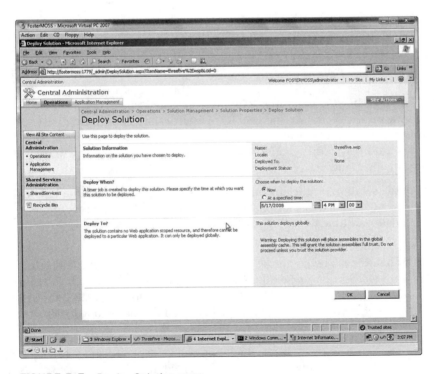

FIGURE B.7   Deploy Solution page.

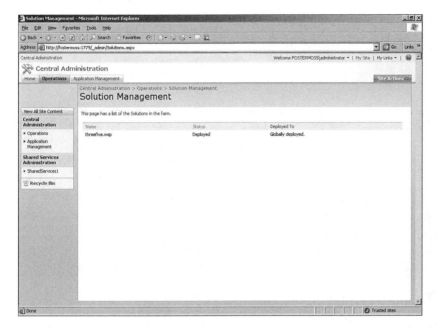

FIGURE B.8   Solution Management page (deployed solution).

Activating the Feature

Now that the solution has been deployed, you must activate the features that were also deployed, which was the point of creating the feature receiver described in Listing B.6. Now is when it is important to remember how your feature was scoped because it will affect where you will go to activate the feature itself.

Because the feature was scoped at the web application level, it will be activated by using the Application Management tab of SharePoint Central Administration. Figure B.9 illustrates the Application Management tab of SharePoint Central Administration and highlights (with a circle) the link that you will need to use to manage web application features.

When you click on the Manage Web Application Features link, you are taken to a page on which you can manage features that are scoped at the web application level. Figure B.10 shows the new ThreeFive feature that has been created and deployed.

All you need to do at this point is click the Activate button and the feature will be enabled for your web application. In this instance, it will simply make the defined updates to the Web.Config file and then restart IIS to complete the activation of the feature.

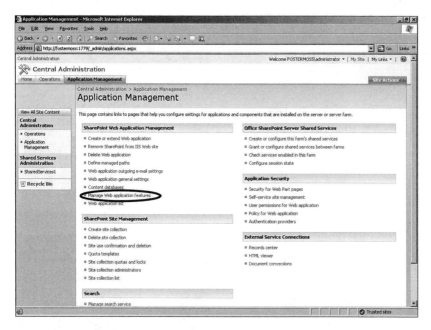

FIGURE B.9   SharePoint Central Administration—Application Management tab.

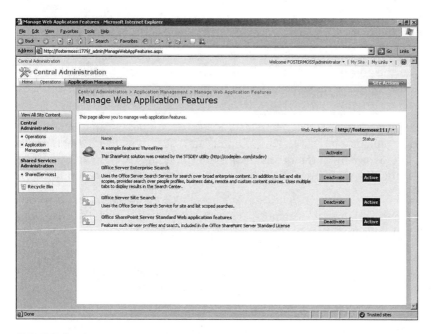

FIGURE B.10   Activating the ThreeFive feature.

Summary

Though this chapter only discusses deploying changes to the Web.Config file, you can deploy many other things to SharePoint and WSS by using a feature, but those are out of the scope of this book. In this chapter, you learned how to create a feature with the STSDev utility and then deploy changes to the SharePoint and WSS Web.Config file. Features offer a standard way to deploy changes to SharePoint and WSS as it gives a more consistent method of deployment and, most important, a way to roll back your changes.

Index

O-P

Q-R

UNLEASHED

Unleashed takes you beyond the basics, providing an exhaustive, technically sophisticated reference for professionals who need to exploit a technology to its fullest potential. It's the best resource for practical advice from the experts, and the most in-depth coverage of the latest technologies.

ASP.NET 3.5 Unleashed
ISBN-13: 978-0-672-33011-7

OTHER UNLEASHED TITLES

C# 3.0 Unleashed
ISBN-13: 978-0-672-32981-4

LINQ Unleashed
ISBN-13: 978-0-672-32983-8

Microsoft Dynamics CRM 4.0 Unleashed
ISBN-13: 978-0-672-32970-8

Microsoft Exchange Server 2007 Unleashed
ISBN-13: 978-0-672-32920-3

Microsoft Expression Blend Unleashed
ISBN-13: 978-0-672-32931-9

Microsoft ISA Server 2006 Unleashed
ISBN-13: 978-0-672-32919-7

Microsoft Office Project Server 2007 Unleashed
ISBN-13: 978-0-672-32921-0

Microsoft SharePoint 2007 Development Unleashed
ISBN-13: 978-0-672-32903-6

Microsoft Small Business Server 2008 Unleashed
ISBN-13: 978-0-672-32957-9

Microsoft SQL Server 2005 Unleashed
ISBN-13: 978-0-672-32824-4

Microsoft Visual Studio 2008 Unleashed
ISBN-13: 978-0-672-32972-2

Microsoft XNA Unleashed
ISBN-13: 978-0-672-32964-7

System Center Operations Manager 2007 Unleashed
ISBN-13: 978-0-672-32955-5

VBScript, WMI, and ADSI Unleashed
ISBN-13: 978-0-321-50171-4

Windows Communication Foundation 3.5 Unleashed
ISBN-13: 978-0-672-33024-7

Windows PowerShell Unleashed
ISBN-13: 978-0-672-32953-1

Windows Server 2008 Hyper-V Unleashed
ISBN-13: 978-0-672-33028-5

Silverlight 2 Unleashed
ISBN-13: 978-0-672-33014-8

Windows Presentation Foundation Unleashed
ISBN-13: 978-0-672-32891-6

SAMS

informit.com/sams

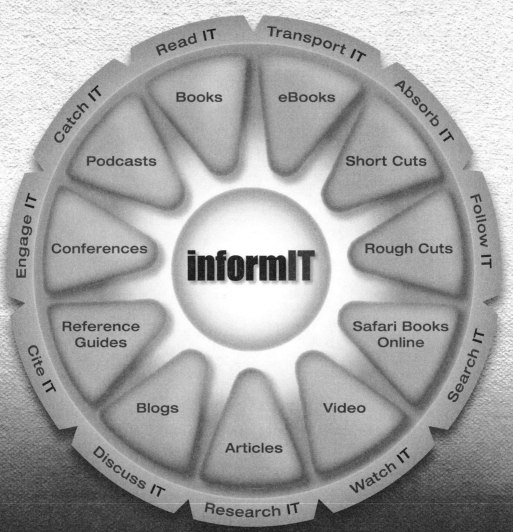

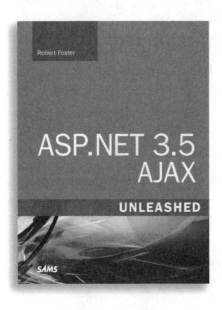

FREE Online Edition

Your purchase of **ASP.NET 3.5 AJAX Unleashed** includes access to a free online edition for 45 days through the Safari Books Online subscription service. Nearly every Sams book is available online through Safari Books Online, along with more than 5,000 other technical books and videos from publishers such as Addison-Wesley Professional, Cisco Press, Exam Cram, IBM Press, O'Reilly, Prentice Hall, and Que.

SAFARI BOOKS ONLINE allows you to search for a specific answer, cut and paste code, download chapters, and stay current with emerging technologies.

Activate your FREE Online Edition at
www.informit.com/safarifree

> **STEP 1:** Enter the coupon code: U2HS-PPPI-SYQX-FSI2-UHQZ.

> **STEP 2:** New Safari users, complete the brief registration form.
> Safari subscribers, just log in.

If you have difficulty registering on Safari or accessing the online edition, please e-mail customer-service@safaribooksonline.com